ALL ABOUT PUPPIES
YOUR DOG'S FIRST YEAR

all about
PUPPIES

YOUR DOG'S FIRST YEAR

by
Bob Bartos
Director, Friskies Research Kennels
Carnation, Washington
and
Elizabeth Hutchings

A SIGNET BOOK

NEW AMERICAN LIBRARY

Drawings: Jimmy Tsuchimori
Design: Angelo Grasso
Inside Photographs: Walter Chandoha

Acknowledgments

This book has been written with the technical assistance of:

Carnation Research Center, Van Nuys, California
  J. M. McIntire, Ph.D., General Manager of Research
  W. S. Claus, Ph.D., Director of Coordination and Planning.
  Lloyd Miller, Ph.D., Director of Pet Food Research
  Milo Nielsen, Ph.D., Manager of Pet Food Products

Carnation Farms, Carnation, Washington
  Erich Studer, D.V.M., Director, Veterinary Research,
    Friskies Research Kennels
  Gene Faltin, Nutritionist, Friskies Research Kennels

John D. Chudacoff, D.V.M., Consultant in Veterinary
  Medicine, Carnation Company, Los Angeles, California

The authors gratefully acknowledge their indebtedness to
Felicia Ames, from whose writings some portions of this
work have been drawn.

Contents

all about
PUPPIES
YOUR DOG'S FIRST YEAR

Chapter 1

THE ART OF MATCHMAKING
(Choose the Right Puppy for You)

So you're going to adopt a puppy. Congratulations! He can grow up to be the best friend you've ever had.

No animal is more lovable, or more loving, than the dog. He is a gentle protector and playmate for children, a superb companion for adults. He is an incomparable pet. But there are some enormous ifs in dog ownership. Let's look at a few of them before you take the plunge.

- Your dog will be with you for a very long time (the average dog lives to be 12 years old, and many live much longer).
- Your dog will become an intimate part of your family household (or he will not be a good pet).
- Your dog will require constant care, companionship and training (or you should not own a dog).
- Not all dogs are suited to all people or all places (and vice versa).

Choosing a pet can be a highly emotional affair. All puppies are appealing, and it's easy to fall for the first set of liquid brown eyes and winning ways you meet. But if you act on impulse, you might regret it later. And so might your dog, if he could only talk. The German Shepherds, St. Bernards and Great Danes confined to city apartments, the delicate Chihuahua who cowers under the bed to avoid well-meant manhandling by the children, the feisty little terrier whose owner thought she was getting a lap dog— these and many more mismatched pets should have their own liberation movement.

The point is that pet ownership is a genuine responsibility, and before you accept this responsibility you should give time and thought to choosing the right pet for you. Ask yourself some of the following questions:

Why do you want a dog? As a companion for children, a solace for loneliness, a household guard, a hunter, a status symbol?

Do you have room for him? If you live in an apartment you should choose a breed that does not require a great deal of exercise. If you live in the suburbs, you should choose a dog that will accept backyard confinement. If you live in the country, your choice is almost unlimited.

Do you have time for him? All dogs need some companionship and play, but the young puppy requires lots of attention. If you're not willing to give it to him and to put up with a certain amount of puppy mischief, you should consider adopting an older dog.

Will he be an outdoor or indoor dog? Some breeds can carpet a house with dog hairs. Others, such as Poodles, Dachshunds, Bulldogs and most of the wire-haired breeds, shed very little.

Do you have small children? You have a wide choice, because most dogs patiently endure the trauma of children. To be fair to both children and dog, however, avoid breeds that tend to be fragile, temperamental or high-strung.

What kind of people do you like? Lively, animated, aggressive, or quiet, relaxed and low-keyed? Dogs have dispositions, too. Remember that you're matchmaking, and select a dog that will suit your own temperament.

The answers to these questions will give you an approximate profile of yourself as a pet owner. Let's say you're a suburban family with two small boys who are long on roughhousing and short on patience. Then you probably should choose one of the sturdy working dogs, hounds or sporting breeds with even dispositions and physical stamina to take rough-and-tumble play. If you're looking for a burglar alarm, you can't do much better than one of the terriers. These lively, alert, aggressive dogs will take on all comers. Terriers adapt well to apartment living, and so do the delightful and decorative toy breeds. Toy dogs make superb companions for adults, but most are too fragile to be suitable pets for young children.

MONGREL OR PUREBRED?

There is a right dog for you, and probably many right choices among the approximately 129 breeds currently recognized by the American Kennel Club. And there are, of course, the mixed breeds —the mutts or mongrels that for many years have been America's favorites. They seem to be on the decline now, perhaps for good reason.

Mongrels can make superb pets, as their loyal owners will testify. But many mongrels grow up to be unattractive, unhealthy and unreliable in disposition. These are the dogs that end up in city pounds and animal shelters by the millions. Unwanted and unloved, most of them must be destroyed. A mongrel may be a risky choice unless you know something about his ancestry. This is not difficult to trace with a crossbreed (a puppy whose dam and sire were different purebreds), but the true mutt bears a motley mixture of genes. Of course, you may be lucky and get the smartest and most lovable dog in the world. But you do have a better chance of getting a pet of predictable size, appearance and temperament by buying a purebred animal.

THE BLUEBLOODS

Purebred dogs are listed by the American Kennel Club under six general groups—sporting dogs, working dogs, hounds, terriers, toys and non-sporting or companion dogs. While there are exceptions in every category, the animals in each of the six groups do share certain general personality traits to help you make your selection. The next two chapters describe some of the characteristics of these six breed categories. The color pictures in the middle of the book show representative members of each group.

Read Chapters 2 and 3 as your introduction to the breeds. Visit dog shows and breeding kennels in your area. And as you narrow your choice down, do some further reading on the breeds you are considering. You'll find ample material at your local library. A little homework on the fascinating subject of dogs can be a lot of fun and very rewarding in making the right choice.

For further information on purebreds, write to the American Kennel Club, 51 Madison Avenue, New York, N.Y. 10010. This organization, which exists to promote fine breed standards, will not recommend a specific kind of dog, but it will put you in touch with reliable breeders in your area.

There are many fine purebred dogs not recognized by the AKC. Some of the great hunting hounds, such as the Bluetick, Redbone and Plott hounds, are listed under a separate registry. England's Cavalier King Charles Spaniel, a court favorite as long as 300 years ago, is not on the AKC list. These and many others (authorities estimate that there are as many as 400 separate breeds throughout the world) are fine blooded animals that have long been recognized in their homelands and are gradually gaining popularity in America.

WHERE TO BUY

Now that you've done your homework, where should you buy your pet? By far the most reliable source is an established breeder or kennel recommended by the AKC or your veterinarian. You can get good dogs from private owners, too, but be sure to investigate both sides of the dog's family tree. The pet shop adds one extra step for a puppy, sometimes a traumatic one, between the comfort of his litter and the adventure of his new home. It is much better to adopt a puppy directly from his own litter. This is not always possible for city dwellers, however. If you buy from a pet shop, make very sure it is a clean, reliable, long-established operation; and take special pains to check out your prospective pet's health and disposition. You can never be too careful.

This is no time for bargain-hunting. A puppy is one purchase that you won't turn in for next year's model, and your initial investment can assure you of a healthy specimen.

Wherever you get your dog, *he should be examined by a veterinarian before final purchase.*

If the kennel provides the examination, ask for a certificate of inoculations and a complete health record signed by a veterinarian. If the dealer does not provide this service, arrange for the examination yourself. This is your best insurance for getting a sound and healthy pup.

In the rare cases where it is not possible to have the pup examined, there are certain signs of health you can look for yourself. Examine his coat for patchy areas, which could be an indication of mange, ringworm or eczema. His eyes and nose should be clear of discharge, and the insides of his ears pink and free from inflammation. Check to see that his teeth are white (discolored teeth may indicate a previous illness), the jaws and teeth aligned, and the gums pink and firm. His stomach should be plump but not greatly distended; a bloated stomach may be a sympton of worms, other parasites, or even of malformation. Crooked or swollen joints could indicate rickets, resulting from poor diet. He should be bright-eyed and have a general appearance of good health.

Watching your prospective pet at play with his littermates will give you a glimpse of his personality. Don't be beguiled by that shy little fellow; his shyness may indicate a neurosis he'll never grow out of. The healthy puppy will be alert and playful.

Dr. Michael Fox, noted veterinarian and authority on canine behavior, has devised some simple behavior tests that you might adapt to give you some clues about your prospective pup's personality.

Watch the litter at feeding time. Nothing brings out the pecking order more clearly than congested traffic on the chow line. The top pups in the hierarchy will get there first, and use growls and threats to keep the others away until they are finished eating. This is a ploy they've learned from their mother, who uses the same menacing sounds to keep her pups away while she finishes her meal in peace. The growlers may be the quick learners; they certainly are indicating some healthy aggression. It doesn't necessarily mean they're bullies; pups aggressive in the litter are often friendly and submissive with people.

Another test is to remove puppy from the litter and isolate him in an unfamiliar place, preferably one without interesting objects to divert his attention. How much and how soon a puppy cries when he's left alone are indications of his emotional stability and confidence. Some pups will crouch and cry immediately; others will explore a bit before sending out a distress signal. The more outgoing the puppy, the more he will explore. Or leave the puppy alone with a colorful, unfamiliar object. If he circles, sniffs and pokes at this strange new thing, he's indicating alertness and healthy curiosity.

Watch the puppies with people, too. Ask a kennel attendant, someone familiar to the puppies, to separate your prospective pet from the litter. When the attendant kneels, watch to see how long the puppy greets him with affectionate licking and tail-wagging. When the attendant walks away, does puppy follow him or does he seem intimidated? When the attendant reaches out with one hand and calls, is the puppy cautious or responsive? If the attendant shouts, claps and pushes puppy away, how quickly does he recover? If he indicates fear but quickly bounces back, he may be more trainable than a puppy who isn't fazed by the threat.

For family life, choose a pup that seems outgoing and responsive to people. Breeders who are familiar with their puppies' personalities should be able to give you some guidance. But do avoid the overly-timid. That little loner may tug at your heartstrings, but remember that extreme shyness can be an indication of illness, a genetic defect, or some trauma in the puppy's early life from which he'll never recover.

If you are buying a purebred, the dealer should give you his AKC registration or a signed, dated bill of sale stating the dog's birth day, sex, color, breed and markings, names and registration numbers of its parents, and the litter registration number.

MALE OR FEMALE

Generalities about the personalities of the male vs. female (bitch) are tricky and always subject to exceptions. As a rule, the female is a little more tractable, easier to handle and train, and more of a homebody than the male. Unless you're going into the business of raising dogs, however, the female should be spayed, an operation that should be performed at between 7 to 10 months of age.

Spaying, incidentally, will not greatly alter your pet's personality or necessarily lead to obesity, all legend to the contrary. It is part of the dog owner's obligation in these days when the pet population explosion has become a matter of national concern. If you choose a female, do not have her bred unless you can guarantee homes for all her offspring.

The male dog is usually more aggressive than the female, more inclined to roam, and tends to make strong one-man attachments. Both make fine pets. Because male dogs are more in demand, they usually cost a little more than females.

HOW OLD

Authorities disagree on the ideal age for adopting a puppy, though they all do agree that the puppy should not be younger than 6 weeks old. Two months is probably about right for puppy's own health and personality development; he's ready by then to leave the litter and join the world of people. If you are investing in a very expensive animal, it might be wise to wait until 4 to 6 months, when he will have received his inoculations and survived the ailments that can attack the very young. But then, no doubt about it, you will have missed a lot of the fun (and hard work) of puppy's first year of life.

Chapter 2

A LOOK AT THE BREEDS—I
(Sporting Dogs, Hounds and Working Dogs)

The American Kennel Club lists six general breed categories: sporting dogs, hounds, working dogs, terriers, toys and non-sporting dogs. A knowledge of the groups is a valuable early guide in selecting a pet. There are fine dogs in all these groups; the important thing is to choose an excellent specimen of the breed you want. Here and in Chapter 3 are the six categories, with brief comments about some of their most popular members:

SPORTING DOGS

English Springer Spaniel
Welsh Springer Spaniel
English Cocker Spaniel
Cocker Spaniel
Sussex Spaniel
Clumber Spaniel
Field Spaniel
Brittany Spaniel
Irish Water Spaniel
American Water Spaniel
English Setter
Irish Setter
Gordon Setter
Pointer
Vizsla
Weimaraner
German Shorthaired Pointer
German Wirehaired Pointer
Wirehaired Pointing Griffon
Golden Retriever
Chesapeake Bay Retriever
Labrador Retriever
Curly-Coated Retriever
Flat-Coated Retriever

The sporting breeds are bird dogs, trained to hunt, point and retrieve both land and water fowl. This calls for intelligence, endurance, adaptability and steady nerves—qualities that many members of this group carry over as household pets. They are, with a few exceptions, very dependable dogs. But remember that they are outdoor animals. Some of these rugged hunters will adapt to the sedentary life; others must have the freedom and space for exercise—and lots of it. Ideally, they *all* should have leg room.

The *Golden Retriever, Labrador Retriever* and the *English Setter*—to name three well-known sporting dogs—are the kind of intelligent, even-tempered, trustworthy animals that make wonderful family pets. Unaggressive by nature, they have calm nerves, sweet dispositions and rugged constitutions; they are ideal companions for active children. The Golden Retriever, in fact, is ranked at the very top in emotional stability by many authorities on canine behavior. He will even adapt to apartment life, but that dense golden coat does shed. All three are relatively large dogs, ranging in size from 55 to 75 pounds. They are better suited for country or suburban living than for crowded city life.

There is, of course, a famous sporting dog whose size is perfect for apartment living. He is the vivacious little *Cocker Spaniel.* The Cocker is a beautiful dog, so appealing and affectionate that it is no wonder he reigned for a record 17 years as America's favorite pet. Popularity can be a hollow crown in the world of dogs, though. In the years when the Cocker was America's top dog, careless breeding practices produced many shy, temperamental and unstable specimens, and the breed went into decline. He is making a comeback now. He is a fine pet for country or city, but be sure to buy from a reliable breeder.

The *Springer Spaniel* is a little bigger and heavier than the Cocker, and probably better able to endure the rough-and-tumble play of children. He is still small enough to be well suited for apartment life. Warm and affectionate with the family, Springers are often wary of strangers and make good watchdogs.

And then there's the *Irish Setter*, one of the most beautiful of all the sporting dogs. Here the question is not so much whether he's the right dog for you, but whether you are the right person for him. Can you rise to this superb animal—to his high spirits, sensitivity and boundless energy? He will lavish affection on you, but you must lavish it back or you'll break his spirit. He needs discipline, but you must be gentle or you'll break his heart. He is, in fact, a bit of a prima donna—beautiful, headstrong, temperamental, entertaining, and inclined to want to run the show. And—no two ways about it—he *must* have exercise.

HOUNDS

Bloodhound
Basset Hound
English Foxhound
American Foxhound
Otterhound
Harrier
Beagle
Black-and-Tan Coonhound
Dachshund
Norwegian Elkhound
Rhodesian Ridgeback
Basenji
Saluki
Whippet
Greyhound
Scottish Deerhound
Irish Wolfhound

Afghan Hound
Borzoi
Ibizan Hound

Hounds are hunters of animals, rather than birds. Some hunt by sight, some by scent. Bred to track down game, most hounds can cover enormous distances without fatigue. And that, for the pet owner, can sometimes be a problem.

Take the case of the *Beagle*, often called the perfect pet for children. The Beagle's virtues read like a Boy Scout's pledge. He is clean, cheerful, courteous, loyal, trustworthy and true. But he is, let's face it, a scent hound, and when the Beagle puts his nose to the ground it can take him miles from home before he even pauses to look up. The Beagle is a roamer. If there is any way to go through, dig under or climb over a backyard fence, he will find it. And an hour or two later you're apt to get a call from a nearby town, asking you to come pick up your dog. But safely confined, even in city apartments, the gentle little Beagle is an ideal family pet. He is sturdy, even-tempered, playful and loving. His short coat is easily cared for, though he does shed. He is inclined to bay when left alone, but this can usually be trained out of him if you attack the problem while he's young (see Chapter 5).

The Beagle's close cousin, the *Basset*, is another hound whose exceptionally amiable disposition makes him an excellent choice for children. He's a bit of a wanderer, too, in spite of those short legs. He'll adjust happily to either city or country, but he needs exercise.

One of the best apartment animals among the

hounds is the Dachshund, for many years one of
the top 10 dogs in the U.S. The Dachshund's
popularity is well deserved. He is small, clean and
sheds very little. And he's packed with personality. The Dachsy loves people; in fact, he thinks
he *is* people, and he fits into family life beau-
tifully, in both city and suburbs.

Another dog ideally suited for city life is the
Basenji. First of all, he is quiet. Though he is
often called "barkless," the Basenji does have a
voice (more like a chortle than a bark), but he
uses it only to express joy. Second, he is clean;
he grooms his short, lustrous coat like a cat. And
finally, he has a happy, playful and intelligent
nature. With his short, erect ears and tightly
curled tail, the Basenji is extremely unhoundlike
in appearance, but his hunting credentials go
back for centuries.

The Beagle, Bassett, Dachshund and Basenji
are small dogs, but there are also some big dogs
in the hound group—in fact, some whoppers! The
tallest and possibly most powerful of all dogs listed by the AKC is the great *Irish Wolfhound.*
This is a magnificent animal of great dignity,
courage and intelligence. He is a fine guard and
companion and a gentle playmate for children,
but he stands three feet tall and weighs as much
as 140 pounds. Almost as huge is the *Scottish
Deerhound,* another colossus who makes a sta-
ble, good-natured family pet. But you'll need
room for these imposing animals.

A bit down the scale in size is the *Black-and-
Tan Coonhound,* one of the great tribe of night
hunters developed in the South for tracking down

possums and raccoons. Relentless on the trail, he is an unaggressive and affectionate pet, ideal for children. So is the granddaddy of them all, the *Bloodhound*. This famous breed, with his legendary scenting instincts, can be traced back many centuries before the birth of Christ. The greatest tracker of all hounds, he is also one of the most tender and loving. Even his name belies his gentle nature; he is called Bloodhound because during the Middle Ages, when he was a favorite of the nobility, the breed's bloodlines were carefully protected. He became the "blooded hound."

These are big dogs, bred to do a job, and they are happiest at work. The dog is infinitely adaptive to man's ways, and even these goliaths will adjust to quiet and confinement. But the hounds, especially the big ones, are far happier and healthier in the country, where they have room to roam.

WORKING DOGS

Collie
Shetland Sheepdog
Old English Sheepdog
Great Pyrenees
Komondor
Puli
Welsh Corgi
Rottweiler
Belgian Sheepdog
Belgian Tervuren
Belgian Malinois
German Shepherd
Briard
Bouvier des Flandres
Standard Schnauzer

Giant Schnauzer
Doberman Pinscher
Mastiff
Bull Mastiff
Great Dane
Boxer
St. Bernard
Bernese Mountain Dog
Kuvasz
Newfoundland
Alaskan Malamute
Samoyed
Siberian Husky
Akita
Bearded Collie

Primitive man first used dog as a hunting companion, but before many eons rolled by he had him hard at work at other jobs. The dog became guard, herder, drover, warrior, draft animal, turnspit and sleuth. The working breeds are a distinguished but motley crew, bred and trained through the ages to be specialists in their own work and environment. Many of them are still working, but many more are family pets.

Two of the most famous dogs in the world belong to the working group—the *German Shepherd* and the *Collie*. To name any one dog as "most intelligent" could start a civil war among dog fanciers, but all authorities would put the German Shepherd well up on the high-IQ list. He is certainly one of the most trainable, as evidenced by his varied roles as seeing-eye guide, war dog, actor, detective, rescuer and guard. These are jobs that require courage, stamina, poise and high intelligence—all qualities with which this animal is superbly endowed.

The German Shepherd is amazing, but he has his faults. Though the breed is not inherently vicious, careless breeding practices with this long-popular dog have produced some unstable and aggressive animals. At best he can be headstrong and needs a firm hand; at his worst he can be dangerous. Also, he is susceptible to hip dysplasia, a crippling joint and bone disorder that affects many of the larger breeds. This, again, can be the result of careless breeding. But these are faults of people, not of the dog. The German Shepherd is incomparable, if you select with care.

The *Collie* is the great shepherd and farm dog of the British Isles. Today's long-nosed aristocrat, bred for beauty and show, is less rugged (and, it has been whispered, less intelligent) than his hard-working Scottish ancestors. But he is a beautiful and graceful animal whose herding and guarding instincts have made him a fabled companion for children. That long coat needs daily grooming, and he needs plenty of exercise. Again, be wary; because of his great popularity, this is another fine animal that has suffered the effects of faulty breeding. The Collie is highly susceptible to eye troubles.

There is a small version of the Collie—the *Shetland Sheepdog* or "Sheltie"—that makes a fine house or apartment pet. He has the same lush coat, so he'll require constant grooming, but his size, sensitive nature and loving ways make him a fine family housepet. He is a spunky little watchdog, too. So is another small herding dog, the

Welsh Corgi. This sturdy short-legged little dog, distant cousin of the Dachshund, loves to guard his household. He's a good size for house or apartment, but he should be exercised frequently.

Bred as they were for hard labor, it's not surprising that the working group includes some giants—the *Great Dane, Mastiff, Newfoundland,* and *St. Bernard.* These enormous dogs are not designed for urban living, even though some are being forced into it and have adjusted very well. The Mastiff, Newfoundland and St. Bernard are gentle, sweet-tempered animals, rather lethargic by nature, who are quite content even with apartment living. But one wag of the tail, and down goes the table lamp. One affectionate nudge, and down goes Junior! These dogs need room.

Chapter 3

A LOOK AT THE BREEDS—II
(Terriers, Toys and Non-Sporting Dogs)

TERRIERS

Scottish Terrier
Skye Terrier
Cairn Terrier
Sealyham Terrier
Lakeland Terrier
West Highland White Terrier
Fox Terrier
Bull Terrier

Dandie Dinmont Terrier
Border Terrier
Staffordshire Terrier
Norfolk Terrier
Norwich Terrier
Australian Terrier
Bedlington Terrier
Airedale Terrier
Irish Terrier
Manchester Terrier
Kerry Blue Terrier
Welsh Terrier
Soft Coated Wheaten Terrier
Miniature Schnauzer
Staffordshire Bull Terrier

Terriers are the spunky little scrappers that for many centuries were the common man's dog. You won't find the terrier's likeness on Egyptian urns or medieval tapestries. While the hound was hunting for the aristocracy, the terrier was ferreting out rodents and catching small game for his humble master. He was lowly and anonymous; he was Everydog. Certainly a humble heritage.

But the terrier has come into his own. For many people, he is the ideal city dog. Most terriers are small. Most of them are wire-haired and shed very little. And they are superb watchdogs. Devoted, cheerful and entertaining in family life, they are suspicious of strangers. And they are absolutely fearless.

But the terrier's aggressive nature has its disadvantages, too. Many terriers are high-strung animals that require a great deal of activity. They are not the type to curl up contentedly at your feet; if you can't give them exercise and attention, they will expend their restless energy in mischief —or barking. Many of the terriers are inclined to be yappers.

As in all the dog groups, there are exceptions. The *Airedale*, largest dog in the group, is not a high-strung animal or a habitual barker. Often called "king of the terriers," he is a friendly, gay and sweet-tempered pet who is highly trainable and good with children. But he has the terrier courage and energy; he should have lots of activity.

Another famous member of the group is the *Fox Terrier*, the stylish and alert little dog that has enjoyed world-wide popularity. There are two strains—smooth and wire-haired. The smooth-coated Fox Terrier is believed to have Greyhound blood in his ancestry, which may account for his graceful, patrician bearing. Both types are sprightly, playful companions, a bit on the noisy side, and inclined to one-man devotion.

With the exception of the German Miniature Schnauzer, all terriers come from the British Isles. Scotland's most famous contribution is the Scottish Terrier (to Americans, the beloved "Scotty") but the Skye, Cairn, West Highland White, Dandie Dinmont and Border terriers also hail from the Highlands.

As all-purpose farm dogs in their homelands, the rough-coated terriers were never noted for their beauty. But styled, clipped and combed they are as stylish and smart as the doggiest of breeds. The *Scotty* is a case in point. At home he was a tough, nervy little hunter with powerful teeth that could make quick work of his quarry. But in the

U.S. his carefully contrived good looks has made him a popular cover dog and a favorite pet. Like most terriers, he is independent, aggressive, one-mannish and fearless.

Another dandy in the group is the dashing *Kerry Blue*, national dog of Ireland. In his native land, where he is used as a terrier, tracker, retriever, shepherd and police dog, his dense, blue-gray coat is never clipped. But in America, where he is a stylish pet and a peerless watchdog, his coat is trimmed and combed to perfection. The Kerry Blue is an exceptionally healthy, long-lived extrovert with a sparkling personality. Like his compatriot, the *Irish Terrier*, he is gung-ho for battle, a bit of a roughneck who is fine with the family but bears watching with outsiders.

TOY DOGS

Toy Poodle
Pomeranian
Papillon
Japanese Spaniel
Pekingese
Maltese
English Toy Spaniel
Pug
Silky Terrier
Shih Tzu
Chihuahua
Affenpinscher
Brussels Griffon
Miniature Pinscher
Toy Manchester Terrier
Italian Greyhound
Yorkshire Terrier

The toys are exactly what the name implies—
dogs bred and shaped to be man's playthings.
They are the miniatures, so small that some can
be carried in the sleeve of a flowing robe, as were
the proud Pekingese in the royal courts of ancient
China.

But in heart, courage and loyal devotion to
their masters, the toys are unsurpassed. One Chihuahua, tiniest dog in the world, even became a
seeing-eye guide when his aged master lost his
sight, proudly leading the way through the bust-
ling street traffic of a California city!

The toys are gallant, independent and extremely sensitive to the moods of those they love. Most
of them are too small and fragile to be suitable
pets for children. In fact, they are a little like
children themselves—spirited, demanding of attention, and adorable. When over indulged they
can even be a bit tyrannical. But for the adult who
wants a constant and devoted companion, you
cannot do better than a toy.

The *Chihuahua* is ideal for apartments. He is
clean, odorless, doesn't shed and he loves to travel
with his master. He's not as fragile as he looks;
in fact, he's one of the most durable of dogs. But
he cannot take cold weather and like many of
the toys, he tends to be domineering and over-
possessive. The Chihuahua is not a pet for children, and neither is the haughty *Pekingese*. The
Peke wears an expression of arrogant disdain, a
reflection perhaps of his royal background. For
many centuries these handsome little dogs were
the most carefully guarded treasures of the Im-
perial Palace at Peking. Only members of the

royal family could own one of these sacred dogs, which were prohibited by law from ever being removed from the confines of the palace.

When the Peke finally did break out in the nineteenth century, he rapidly became a world-wide favorite. He is a very decorative and stylish pet, but that lion-like coat calls for constant brushing and combing. He needs little exercise, and he is an entertaining individualist. He is not friendly to outsiders and, like many short-nosed breeds, he tends to have breathing problems.

Another Oriental aristocrat is the *Pug*. Never noted for his beauty, he was nevertheless the darling of international society in the days of bustle and barouche. The Pug might be due for a comeback. If you don't mind his comic-valentine appearance, he has many virtues for modern living. He is clean, odorless, doesn't shed, needs little grooming, and he is not as excitable and demanding as many of the toys.

The *Maltese, Papillon,* and *Pomeranian* are all beautiful toys who demand much pampering and primping. Intelligent, animated and devoted, they are wonderful company; but they do insist upon attention, and those gorgeous coats call for long and loving beauty treatments every day. The all-out champion in this respect is probably the *Yorkshire Terrier*, who spends half his life in endless grooming of his beautiful coat. But his devoted followers say that this lovable little companion is worth every minute of it.

And, after all, there are lots of people who want just that—someone to pamper and pet. The toys are ideal for them. They ask for lots of love and attention, and they give it back a thousandfold.

NON-SPORTING DOGS

Poodle
Dalmation
Bulldog
French Bulldog
Boston Terrier
Chow Chow
Keeshond
Schipperke
Lhasa Apso
Bichon Frise
Tibetan Terrier

The non-sporting breeds are an arbitrary selection of dogs that once were workers or hunters, but are now pets. They have little in common except that they are individualists and they include the most individualistic and most popular dog in the world —the Poodle.

The *Poodle* has charisma. He is endlessly entertaining, loves attention and is almost human is his expression and tastes. He is so intelligent and responsive that he can be trained to do almost anything—except, perhaps, to be quiet and retiring. He is high-spirited and a born ham; he accepts the elaborate haircuts, painted toenails, and bejeweled collars that have become his lot in modern society with poise and theatrical flair.

The Poodle is anything but effete, however. Originally a rugged water retriever, the Standard Poodle is still a strong and healthy animal that loves vigorous activity. He is a good companion for active children. His wiry coat does not shed, but it grows very fast and must be clipped and groomed frequently. A fine family pet for city or country, but remember that the Poodle is a presence; he demands attention. And the Poodle, too, has suffered from his long reign as America's top dog. Buy from a reliable breeder.

Another glamour dog in the group is the *Lhasa Apso*, one of the beautiful "lion dogs" that have been imported to America from the Orient. Originally an indoor watchdog in the temples of Tibet, he is still an alert guard, playful and loving with his master but suspicious of strangers. He is small and needs little exercise, but his gorgeous long coat calls for constant care.

The *Boston Terrier* is one of the dogs often singled out as ideal for city living; indeed, he was bred for city life. He is small, quiet, has no body odor, sheds very little, and is easily trained. This little blueblood, one of the few American breeds, originated in Boston in the late nineteenth century. By 1900 he had climbed to the list of America's top 10 favorites, there to reign for an incredible 63 years. A wonderful companion, he is courteous and responsive to his master's every mood. But like most short-nosed breeds he is inclined to drool and snore. The females have difficulty during whelping; a large percentage of Boston Terrier puppies are caesarian born.

The *Bulldog* looks terrifying, but he's not mad at anybody. You could not find a pet more tender and peace-loving than this burly dog. Of course, this was not always so. The Bulldog's flattened-out nose and undershot jaw, his grotesquely bowed legs and barrel chest were all shaped for the cruel sport of bullbaiting. The aggressiveness has been bred out of him, but he's left with some uncomfortable physical legacies. With his pushed-in nose, he is inclined to have breathing problems; the bulldog snores, wheezes, snorts and drools. The breed has difficulty in whelping and is short-lived—one more result of man's genetic tampering. The Bulldog hasn't lost his nerve; he's still a good watchdog. But he is reliable and gentle with children and is completely content with a quiet, inactive life.

·One of the best country dogs in the group is the *Dalmatian*, the handsome coach dog that looks as if he just stepped out of a Currier and Ives print. The Dalmatian's short coat requires virtually no grooming, and he is hardy enough for any climate. But the quiet life is not for him. The Dalmatian is an intelligent, playful and entertaining companion, but he thrives best with freedom and lots of exercise.

Chapter 4

OFF TO A GOOD START
(Puppy's First Day)

Good starts are important, and puppy begins being a member of your family on the day he arrives in your house. This is the biggest adventure of his life. He's separated for the first time from his mother and littermates—and he misses them. He is suddenly out in the great big world— and he's a little scared.

How this adventure goes depends very much on you. If you make a few simple preparations for his arrival, and are calm, quiet and reassuring during his first day, he'll adapt quickly. But if you make this an occasion for riotous celebration, you could find yourself with a nervous pup on your hands. Treat this newcomer gently, as you would a baby. After all, that's what he is.

GETTING READY

Before you bring your new pet home, lay in a supply of Friskies Puppy Food, a special formula for growing pups, and a few possessions that will be exclusively his own. He will need a bed, food and water bowls and a collar. A chewable, hard rubber toy would be a nice welcoming extra.

Dog beds are available in vast array these days, ranging from the practical to the ridiculous. You can buy beribboned baskets with satin pillows, "puptents" in decorator colors, even beds padded with mink or chinchilla. But you'd do best to avoid the gag and gimmicks. What you want for puppy is a bed that will provide warmth, comfort and protection. It can be home-made or store-bought, but it must meet certain standards:

- The bed should be raised a few inches off the floor, or well padded to protect puppy from chills.
- It should be placed in a warm and quiet spot, completely protected from drafts. Drafts are very dangerous to puppies, because of their low resistance to infection.
- It should be kept clean, as another precaution against disease.
- Ideally, it should have a roof or door, or sides too high to jump or climb over, in order to keep puppy confined until he's housebroken.

- It should be made of a sturdy material that puppy can't chew into shreds.

One of the most practical and convenient beds, recommended by many dog trainers, is a shipping or show crate, available in pet shops. A crate will meet all puppy's needs for privacy and protection, and it will also come in handy when you want to transport him by car. If you don't want to invest in a crate, you can construct one by putting a heavy-duty wire mesh lid or door on a wooden box; make sure the box provides adequate ventilation.

Another way to improvise a puppy bed is to use a child's playpen. A blanket secured over the top of one end of the playpen makes a cozy sleeping den, and there's still plenty of play space. The playpen offers obvious advantages during puppy's chewing and puddling periods. But you must make sure he can't escape through the bars; if he's a very tiny pup you probably should attach some kind of metal screening to the outside of the pen.

Whatever kind of bed you choose, pad it well with a thick, flat layer of newspapers, which can be changed as soon as they become soiled. Cover the newspapers with something soft like an old blanket or towel, and place the bed in a quiet, draft-free corner, well apart from family traffic or hubbub. But don't isolate him in a closed room at the beginning, when he's still a newcomer to your household. Dogs are social animals, and the ordinary sounds of family life will be comforting to the new puppy.

Make it a rule that when puppy is sacked in,

his bed is off limits to all intruders. Nothing is more important to his growth, energy and emotional stability than long periods of peaceful, uninterrupted sleep.

OUTDOOR KENNELS

The pup that is going to be raised as an outdoor animal can start sleeping in a kennel at around 3 to 4 months (or even younger during the summer months). This is true of large and medium-sized dogs only; small dogs should sleep indoors longer. Toy breeds should not be kenneled outdoors under any circumstances.

Doghouses can be plain or fancy. You can build one from scratch, assemble one of the pre-fab jobs from your local pet dealer, or buy one ready-made. Friskies Research Kennels recommends a few simple standards that the outdoor kennel should meet for your pet's health and comfort:

It must be dry and draft-free. The floor should be raised a few inches off the ground so that no dampness can get in, and it should be covered with a soft bedding material. Place the doghouse in a spot that provides both shade and protection from the winds. The doorway should be covered with a baffle or canvas flap, and the roof or one side should be removable for easy cleaning.

An outdoor kennel must be suited to the climate. Choose a material—plywood, cinder or concrete block, brick, and so on—to match the weather puppy will be exposed to. In warm areas, a single-thickness roof that can be tilted for ventilation is excellent, as are windows that are hinged. In cold areas, double-thick or insulated roofs should be used. A removable louvered section inserted between the roof and the sleeping quarters will allow air circulation in warm weather; remove the louvered section during cold weather to aid in heating the house. If the house is wood, paint it both inside and out to discourage parasites. Keep it clean; dogs are clean by nature, so you should help your pet by doing a regular doghouse cleaning.

As a rule, dogs are happier and more affectionate and companionable pets if they are allowed to live indoors, close to family activity. But whichever way it is to be, indoors or out, be consistent. Healthy puppies can adapt to either arrangement, but sudden changes in temperature or great extremes of temperature are hard on them. A spell of near-zero weather is a signal to move your dog to a warmer spot for a while. And remember that dogs suffer terribly from unrelieved sun and extreme heat; a shady, cool spot must always be available in the warmer weather.

HIS POSSESSIONS

Puppy's food and water bowls should be of a non-breakable (and non-chewable) material that is easy to keep clean. Metal, hard rubber or plastic are suitable. The food pan should be shallow, so that he can easily get his muzzle into it. As for the water bowl, the cardinal rule is to keep it filled with fresh, cool water at all times. Dogs need a great deal of water and suffer genuine anguish without it, so never let his well run dry.

Get him an inexpensive collar to start with, because he'll soon outgrow it. A soft, flat leather one is suitable for a young pup. Fasten it snugly, with enough room for your finger to slip between it and puppy's neck. He may scratch and paw at it for a while, but he'll soon surrender to this first form of restraint. And he must, because soon you will be attaching a license tag, your proof of legal ownership of your pet, to his collar.

Your local humane society or animal shelter can tell you your city's regulations on dog licenses and where to obtain them. Six months is the deadline in most cities, but some require licensing at an earlier age. You will have to show proof of rabies inoculation, and the license will be renewable annually.

Once the tag is securely fastened to his collar, make it a rule never to remove it. This is his legal identification and your best guarantee of getting him back if he is lost or stolen. A metal tag giving your own name, address and telephone number is a good extra precaution, but don't put your pet's name on it. This could help the dog thief to make friends, and might even be used as evidence if the thief should claim ownership in court.

HIS FIRST DAY

If possible, bring your new pet home in the morning. This will give him a full day to get used to his new world before you put him down for the night. If you have a long car ride, take a padded box along, or better yet, someone to hold and comfort him. Be prepared for accidents by arming yourself with a few newspapers and paper towels or mop-up cloths.

If there are children in your family, their introduction to puppy is one of the most important good starts of all. "Will the dog be all right around children?" is one of the most common queries of the prospective dog owner. But in many cases, the question should be reversed: "Will the children be all right around the dog?"

Children and dogs take naturally to each other, and youngsters can learn some eloquent lessons in devotion and loyalty from even the tiniest pup. But children should also learn some lessons in responsibility and tenderness in the care of pets. One of the easiest ways to teach kindness is to give the children certain tasks of puppy care, such as seeing that he is fed on time, that his water dish is always full, and that his coat is brushed and combed regularly.

Most of all, they should be taught that puppies are fragile. Children, especially very young ones, can sometimes love so much that it hurts. In fact, many experts feel that children under six years of age should not have a small puppy as a pet. They're too inclined to treat all cuddly creatures as if they were teddy bears. Rough handling, tight hugs and falls from beds, sofas, chairs and tables can damage delicate bones. Like human infants, the very young puppy has a soft spot on the top of his head that, if punctured in a fall or rough play, can even cause death.

Here are some play-safe rules for children and every member of the family:

- Never grab a puppy by his front legs. His legs aren't strong enough to take such treatment. And *never* pick him up by the scruff of the neck. Lift him by placing one hand under his chest, the other under his rump, to make him feel secure.

- Don't frighten the young puppy with sudden loud noises.
- Never tease; you want to gain his confidence.
- Never leave him on a high place, even for a moment; he may take a bone-breaking nose-dive.
- Don't overtire a puppy. Cuddling and play-time are good for him, but for brief periods only.
- Never disturb him while he's eating. And don't romp and play with him after his meal; he should have a little quiet time after eating.
- Never, never disturb him while he's sleeping. Like all babies, he needs his sleep, so puppy's naptime must be sacred.

It's a good idea to keep visitors to a minimum on his first day. There will be plenty of time to show him off later. Stand back and let him nose around the house at his own speed; this is his way of establishing his new territorial rights. And remember to put him in his crate often for naps.

WHEN YOUNG MEETS OLD

If your household already has a pet—a cat, perhaps, or an older dog—then you may have a delicate job of introduction on your hands.

Puppy, of course, is a happy little innocent who will head straight for Tabby to find out what this interesting creature is all about. He may get his answer in a scratched nose, hurt feelings and, at the worst, a lifelong fear or hatred of cats. An older dog is apt to be more tolerant of puppy and even enjoy playing with him. But don't count on it. He may be jealous of this newcomer that is invading *his* house and getting all *your* attention.

So you'd better keep a careful eye on both animals, young and old, at the beginning. If it looks as if there's going to be a war of wills, don't decide to stand back and let the fur fly. And don't cradle puppy protectively in your arms while the older animal hisses or barks at your feet. This approach poses a double threat to the older pet; he thinks he's losing *both* home and master.

It's not a bad idea to keep the two pets separated for the first few hours, while puppy explores his new territory. Put the older animal in a closed-off room or in the garden. Old Bowser or Tabby will pick up puppy's scent soon enough and may protest with frantic barking, yowling or scratching at the door, but at least he's been made aware of puppy's presence.

After a while, let the two animals see each other, still separated by some household barricade such as a glass or screen door. By now the older pet's anxiety is beginning to turn into curiosity. The next step is to bring them together. To be on the safe side, there should be two people in the room—one to hold puppy and one to grab the older animal in case he decides to take a flyer at the intruder. It's more likely there'll be nothing more than a few sound effects and a little circling and sniffing until they become fast friends or settle down in cautious resignation.

When your older pet does accept the new puppy, he'll probably become his most loyal playmate and protector. Two animals in a household are almost always happier, more independent, less demanding than the single pet. Not only do they give each other constant companionship, but they recognize themselves as animals and you as people, an important distinction not always clear to the pampered one-and-only.

FIRST DAY FEEDING

Give your puppy frequent light feedings on his first day. Four meals are about right for the pup of three months or younger, three for the older pup. Find out what he's been accustomed to eating, and serve him the same fare for the first day or two. Then you can start gradually introducing the foods that will comprise his regular growth diet (for detailed instructions on puppy feeding, see Chapter 6). Leave him alone while he's eating, give him a good 15 minutes to finish, and then remove his dish. No snacks or tidbits; these can cause stomach aches. And don't forget to put fresh water into the bowl regularly.

FIRST DAY TRAINING

Immediately after every meal, take puppy outdoors or place him on some newspapers. Then hope for the best. Housebreaking should start at once (for instructions, see Chapter 5), even though it may be several weeks before puppy understands the rules of the game. But if you make it a practice to take him outside or place him on papers as soon as he wakes up and after every meal, you're on the right track.

HIS FIRST NIGHT

Some puppies go through their first night in strange surroundings without a whimper, but some get the bedtime blues. The puppy is a cuddler, and he misses the comforting warmth of the litter. If he cries, put a hot-water bottle (not *too* hot) or a wrapped mason jar filled with warm water in his bed for him to snuggle up to. Some veterinarians suggest a ticking clock in his bed, to sound like his mother's heartbeat. A light from a nearby room or the soft sounds from a transistor radio placed near his bed are also good puppy pacifiers.

If he still whimpers, don't scold or punish him. But don't give in to him, either; you want to win this first small war of wills. It's all right to reassure him with comforting pats and quiet words, but don't let him out of his crate. Put him back gently but firmly, and ride it out. He'll soon tire of complaining and fall into the sleep that comes naturally to the young.

And the next morning chances are he will have forgotten that he ever lived anywhere else. He's *your* dog now!

Chapter 5

AS THE TWIG IS BENT...
(Early Puppy Training)

The first year of a dog's life is the equivalent of his infancy and childhood. At the end of that year he is, in human terms, 15 years old—still a bit wet behind the ears perhaps, but on the brink of adulthood. That's why the first year, and especially the first six months, are the pivotal period in a dog's development.

In other words, this is your big chance to shape your pup into the kind of pet you want him to be. Don't let that chance go by; his puppyhood will never come back. Like a child, he needs lots of love, fondling, play and companionship. He also needs discipline. A den animal by nature, the dog looks for a pack leader. If he doesn't get it from you, he'll take it over himself, and you may end up with a spoiled and overindulged household tyrant.

But the dog is also the most marvelously trainable of all animals. He'll do anything to please you, if you make your instructions clear, simple and consistent. He is so trusting, loving and uncritical of his human companions that the dog is often used by psychologists as therapy for disturbed children. He is, in truth, a wonderful best friend. But don't forget that you're the leader in this friendship.

Formal obedience training (see Chapter 10) should not start until your pet is at least six months old. The young pup is too frisky, curious and playful to undergo such rigorous discipline, and if you put too many restraints on his natural instincts for play you could intimidate him for life. But good habits—and bad—do get established early. Take a tip from the mother wolf, who gives her cubs infinite affection, but also makes it clear who's boss in the den.

This chapter will give you some guidelines for establishing good behavior patterns in the young pup. Early training will take some discipline on your part, too. Puppies are so appealing that it's easy to fall into the isn't-he-cute or the just-this-once trap. Don't give in. Teach him not to get up on the furniture, not even just this once. Put him down immediately, and every time, with a stern and disapproving "No!" Don't let him beg at table, no matter how cute he looks; it won't be cute when he's older.

Be firm, gentle and consistent as you make the rules clear. You want to gain his confidence; learning cannot take place without trust. *Never* strike a puppy. Experts at Friskies Research Kennels advise that striking a dog, and especially a very young dog, accomplishes nothing. A stern scolding is punishment enough, and your praise and approval his greatest reward.

FIRST WORDS

If you haven't already chosen a name for him, do so now. Make it short, one that you can call out easily and that he will recognize quickly. And remember that he won't be a puppy forever, so avoid the cute or the comical. If Lassie had been named Lollipop, would she still be a star? Cuddles might be just the word for your pup right now, but a little embarrassing to a grown dog.

Call him by name frequently, especially at mealtime. He won't always respond at first, but one of those times he'll look at you with a bright "Who me?" expression on his face. He's had his first vocabulary lesson.

THE FIRST ETIQUETTE LESSON

You won't need any reminders about housebreaking; the first puddle on the floor will be your starting signal. A crate is the greatest aid in house-training. Start off by always keeping your pup in his crate during the night; don't even let him have a bathroom area to roam about in. When he gets up, take him at once to the papers or to the outdoors, depending on which kind of training you are using (instructions below). Later, when elimination routine has been established, the crate door can be left open. Puppy will go in during the day to rest, and most of the time beat you to bed at night.

There are two ways to accomplish housebreaking—outdoor training and paper training. If your dog is going to use the outdoors eventually, it's much better to start training him to the backyard from the beginning. Some dogs, trained to paper as puppies, have difficulty changing their habits later. But outdoor training is obviously impractical if you have to sprint down several flights of stairs or through halls and elevators to get to the street. In that case you'll have to resort to papers, at least as a starter, and for city dweller this method does have its advantages in times of illness or bad weather. So size up your own situation and take your choice. Here's how:

OUTDOOR TRAINING

Dogs are clean by nature and will not soil their own beds. Dogs return to their own odors. These two canine characteristics are valuable aids in housebreaking. If puppy makes a mistake in the house, as he's bound to in the beginning, mop it up with a cloth and then anchor that cloth outdoors in the spot you've chosen as his special place. As soon as puppy wakes in the morning and after naps, immediately take him to that spot. Do the same after meals, at bedtime, and whenever you see him sniffing the floor or circling.

He'll detect the urine odor in the cloth long after it's dried out. When he performs properly, praise him, pat him, tell him what a fine fellow he is. After a few successes you can remove the cloth. It won't take long for him to understand the purpose of those trips to the backyard, and one fine day he'll scratch at the door to tell you he'd like to step outside. Victory!

PAPER TRAINING

Keep puppy confined to one room, and carpet a sizable area of that room with a thick layer of newspapers, well separated from his bed. Show him what is expected of him by placing him on the papers frequently—always after sleeping, following meals, at bedtime and whenever you see the familiar warning signals. Praise him when he performs well; when you catch him in a mistake, scold him with a firm "No!" and place him on the papers. Following the same principles as in outdoor training, it's a good idea to keep a damp paper on top of the pile during the early stages of training. And be sure to scrub all mistake spots with a strong disinfectant to remove odors. As you see signs of progress, gradually cut down on the size of the papered area until, in time, there is one well-padded place that puppy goes to without error.

As puppy gets older and can restrain himself for longer periods, you can begin taking him out on the street. If he has trouble graduating from indoors to out, you may have to take a paper with you a few times, but it's more likely that the odors from other dogs will tell him what to do. Keep him on a leash, and do not let him relieve himself on sidewalks or lawns. *Curb him.*

Patience and praise are your watchwords during housebreaking. No spankings, and never resort to the old cure of rubbing puppy's nose in the mess—a disgusting and totally ineffective punishment. And finally, discipline works only if it comes at the moment of the crime. Puppy has a short memory, and if you scold him several minutes later he simply won't understand. But he does want to please you. Be patient. If you make your lessons clear and simple, he'll do his best to give a spotless performance.

NERVOUS WETTING

There is one kind of chronic piddling problem, common to puppies and even to some older dogs, that is completely involuntary. It is usually caused by extreme emotion, either ecstasy or fear. You come home after an absence, puppy waddles up to greet you in great excitement, squats at your feet and urinates. Or you pick up his leash and he joyfully scrambles around over the prospect of a walk, leaving a small stream in his path. A stranger appears at the door, looms over puppy, then suddenly swoops down to pat him. Puppy cringes—and wets the carpet.

This is nervous urinating. With proper handling, puppy will outgrow the habit. What happens is that the sphincter, the muscle that closes the bladder, relaxes under extreme excitement. It is not a voluntary action, so punishment will do no good at all; it could even worsen the problem. Instead, try to cool your homecoming greetings a bit. Don't bend down to pat him. Speak to him calmly and affectionately, but walk right past him and give him a little time to settle down. Then kneel to his level and call him to you for some reassuring pats. Ask strangers not to bend over puppy, but to ignore him and let him take the first steps toward making friends. All he needs is to gain a little maturity and self-confidence.

LEASHBREAKING

While you're outdoor training your pup, you can also introduce him to the leash. Don't expect too much. It will be a long time before you start teaching him to heel smartly on lead, but he should get accustomed to the leash at an early age.

After he's done his duty outdoors, attach a lightweight rope or cord to his collar and let him drag it around a bit. When he starts back to the house, pick up the end of the rope loosely and walk with him. Don't drag or yank; he must associate the leash with pleasure. After you've done this a few times, give him a gentle tug on the leash when you start back to the house, speak to him by name and say "Come." Puppy will soon come to like this little exercise; to him it's like holding hands.

BREAKING BAD HABITS

In puppies, bad habits are often simply a matter of doin' what comes naturally. That's why it's hard for the pet owner to recognize the beginning of bad behavior, and even harder to be firm and consistent about correcting it. But those merry little ways can become a pain in the neck all too soon, and it's much easier to prevent bad habits from getting started than to break them later. Here are some common puppy ploys to watch for, and to correct:

Jumping up on people. This is puppy's joyful way of greeting, and he can be very appealing as he dances on his hind legs, his little paws flailing awkwardly until they land on your knees or nylons. Don't be beguiled and don't let your friends encourage him, because jumping up will become a very annoying habit as he gets older. The classic way to break it is to raise your knee just as he jumps, so that he'll bump against it and lose his balance. Another method is to step firmly (but not hard enough to hurt) on his hind feet. If you have a very stubborn dog, simply catch his paws and upset him. These methods are effective with fairly large pups; with smaller ones, grab the front paws and place them on the ground as you sternly scold "No!" or "Down!"

Barking. It's a dog's nature to sound an alert at approaching danger, but if he persists after you've told him to stop he may become a habitual barker. You must not let this happen. In a crowded world where people and their pets occupy close quarters, noisy dogs are a major social nuisance. One beleagured family became so irritated with a neighborhood dog's nighttime cacophony that they made a tape of his incessant barking and played it back to his owners, full volume. In some cities you're liable to a fine if your dog disturbs the peace with habitual barking.

The time to attack the problem is during puppy-hood; the barking habit can be a tough one to break in the adult dog. Let puppy sound his warning signals for a few seconds, then reassure him with a few calming words ("It's all right, Andy"). He's done *his* job, and you've responded. If he continues to bark excitedly, speak directly to him with a commanding "Quiet!" If he still doesn't get the idea, demonstrate by holding his mouth closed for a moment. Remember that you're teaching, not punishing, so don't further excite him by yelling or hitting him. If he doesn't respond, douse him in the face with a little water as you command "Quiet!" This is effective shock treatment, but usually necessary only in extreme cases, when a pup is in a frenzy of barking.

A few lessons like this, *consistently* applied, will do the trick with almost all dogs. If your pet still seems to be developing the barking habit, look for the cause. Is he nervous? Nervous puppies need lots of love and reassurance. Don't bark excitedly back at him; he may think you sense danger, too. Is he underexercised? Highly energetic and aggressive breeds need lots of activity and playtime. Is he lonely? Dogs that are alone too much sometimes bark out of boredom. If you can't spend more time with him, a second animal —another dog, a cat, even a bird—may serve as a quieting companion.

Solitary Silence. You can train your puppy to stay alone in the home without barking. Put him in a room with some of his toys and say "Quiet." Then shut the door and go away, far enough that he doesn't catch your scent. If he starts to howl or bark, go back immediately and scold him sternly. Usually verbal punishment is enough, but if he begins his commotion when you leave again, bang loudly on the door as you say "No" or "Quiet." After ten minutes of silence, let him out and be sure to praise him for his good behavior. Repeat this exercise many times, gradually increasing the period you stay away. But don't be gone too long, or he'll get anxious.

Use the same training, with slight variations, if puppy is a backyard dog. Pound loudly on his kennel roof or on the back door to shock him into silence, and use the water treatment if he persists.

Puppy should learn two simple lessons from this training: that he is expected to be quiet when -he is alone, and that you will always come back and praise him for good conduct. Don't ever let him down on your part of the contract.

Nipping. Puppies chew on everything — even people. It's perfectly natural, when you or the children romp and play with your pup, for him to get overexcited and sink his teeth into pantlegs and socks. You'd better correct him; he might start sinking them into flesh. If he starts growling and nipping during play, stop immediately. Hold him in place or lift him off the ground, look directly at him, and give him a firm and quieting scolding. Then make up with him and start your game again. If he starts getting too rough, stop again and speak to him sternly to slow him down. But don't get angry or overexcited yourself; playtime and even a little roughhousing are natural and good for young animals. You simply want to curb overly aggressive behavior.

Stay. "Stay" is one of the commands you will teach your dog when you begin formal obedience training. You can give him a preschool lesson in this by teaching him to sit quietly when you're preparing his dinner. His natural impulse, of course, is to dash for the food bowl the instant you put it down. Say "No" or "Stay," hold him in place for a moment or two, and then say "All right, Andy" as his signal to go. Do this consistently at morning and evening mealtime. He's learning an important lesson here: to sit quietly until you, the leader, give him the signal to move.

AND A LOT OF LOVE

Let's look once more at the other, and equally important, side of early puppy training—building his trust and self-confidence. Babies need love. This truism applies to all animals, and nothing will help create a healthy, happy disposition in your pet as much as the security of your affection. Scientific studies have shown that dogs denied human handling during a critical period in their development—between the age of 3 and 12 weeks —may be permanently fearful of people.

Give your pup lots of attention. Play with him, walk with him, fondle and pet him. Create a rich learning environment by giving him opportunities to explore and acquaint himself with new places, people and things. And above all, praise him. Praise works wonders with dogs. If puppy gets lots of it from you, he'll learn to enjoy training. And so will you.

Chapter 6

THE PATH TO VITALITY
(How to Feed a Growing Pup)

Puppies are always hungry—and with good reason. They are growing at a fantastic rate (some breeds increase their weight by as much as ten times during the first ten months of life), and they are developing the bone structure, muscle and fat that will quite literally shape their future.

Puppies are also notoriously adept at getting their own way. If you respond to every cute trick with a snack reward, you can easily spoil your pup into a case of malnutrition. Set up a sensible feeding schedule early and stick to it. You'll have a healthier dog and a happier household.

FEED HIM OFTEN

A growing puppy requires two to three times as much food per pound of body weight as an adult dog. His small stomach can't handle large servings (puppy doesn't know this; that's why he's inclined to upchuck), so you'll have to feed him frequently. Under 3 months of age he should have four small meals every day—morning, noon, late afternoon and bedtime. At around 3 months you can drop the late feeding, but keep him on three meals until he is at least 6 months old. From 6 months to a year, give him two meals, morning and evening. By one year of age most dogs are satisfied with a single daily feeding.

You will gradually increase the size of his servings, of course (see feeding chart, page 56). There are bound to be individual variations in this feeding schedule. Dogs reach maturity at somewhere between 10 and 12 months. Some thrive on one meal a day as early as 10 months, others do better on twice-daily feedings all their lives. The amount of exercise your pet gets, the climate, whether he lives indoors or out, his own temperament and many other variables can affect his appetite.

As a general rule, a puppy should be offered as much food as he will eat, unless he's a compulsive overeater or starts developing an unhealthy bulge around the midriff. But most dogs are pretty good self-pacers on food intake, and puppies do need lots of food—*good* food—to meet their enormous growth and energy requirements.

AN ALBUM OF PUPPIES
by Chandoha

BLOODHOUND

BEAGLES

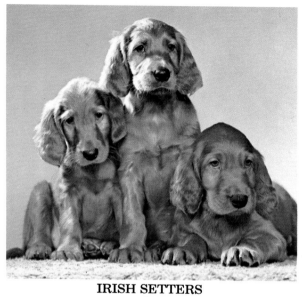

IRISH SETTERS

POODLE

BASSET

SEALYHAM TERRIER

SILKY TERRIER

SAINT BERNARD

DACHSHUND AND COLLIE

MIXED BREEDS

GERMAN SHEPHERDS

COCKER

GREAT DANES

DALMATIANS

MIXED BREEDS

GOLDEN RETRIEVERS

MIXED BREEDS

PEKINGESE AND CHIHUAHUA

MINIATURE SCHNAUZERS

AIREDALE AND FOX TERRIERS

FEED HIM WELL

What is good food for a puppy? The all-important element in his diet is *balance*. Dogs have specific food requirements; they need 43 separate nutrients to achieve a balanced diet. Nutrients are classified as macro- or micronutrients (or in layman's language, major or minor nutrients). Protein, fats, carbohydrates, fiber, water, calcium and phosphorus are macronutrients. Vitamins and minerals are micronutrients. All are equally important. A growing puppy must have all the required nutrients in his diet; if one is missing, a nutritional deficiency will develop.

That is why the foods that he eats are so crucial during a puppy's first year of life. This is the formative period: his nervous system, bone structure, musculature and body condition are developing. Inadequate diet can upset this development and not only retard growth but result in serious skeletal deformities in the adult dog.

Balance is the key word. We know, for instance, that a puppy needs some fat in his diet. Too little fat can lead to dry, scaly skin and a dull, coarse coat; too much will lead to obesity and all its attendant health problems. He needs carbohydrates for bulk and energy, but only in proportion. He must have protein, but that doesn't mean you should put him on a diet of sirloin steak. Meat alone, unless it is fortified with other essential nutrients, would be deficient. It is so lacking in calcium, for example, that a 20-pound dog would have to eat 44 pounds of raw meat daily to get his required amount of the major nutrients.

COME 'N GET IT® Dry Dog Food
Recommended Daily Feeding Amounts for Puppies
(using Come 'N Get It exclusively)

Size Category	Expected Adult Weight	6-10 Wks.	11-16 Wks.	17-28 Wks.	27-52 Wks.
Toy Shih Tzu	12 lbs.	1 cup	1¼ cups	1⅓ cups	1¾ cups
Small Beagle Cocker Spaniel	25 lbs.	1½ cups	2½ cups	2¾ cups	3½ cups
Medium Brittany Spaniel Dalmation	50 lbs.	2⅓ cups	3⅔ cups	5½ cups	7 cups
Large Golden Retriever German Shepherd	100 lbs.	3⅓ cups	5½ cups	7½ cups	9½ cups
Giant Great Dane St. Bernard	175 lbs.	5¾ cups	9½ cups	13 cups	16 cups

MIGHTY DOG® *Canned Dog Food*
Recommended Daily Feeding Amounts For Puppies
(using Mighty Dog exclusively)

Size Category	Expected Adult Weight	6-10 Wks.	11-16 Wks.	17-26 Wks.	27-52 Wks.
Toy					
Shih Tzu	12 lbs.	1½ cans	1¾ cans	2 cans	2½ cans
Small					
Beagle	25 lbs.	2¼ cans	3¾ cans	4 cans	5 cans
Cocker Spaniel					
Medium					
Brittany Spaniel	50 lbs.	3½ cans	5½ cans	8 cans	10 cans
Dalmation					
Large					
Golden Retriever	100 lbs.	5 cans	8 cans	11 cans	14 cans
German Shepherd					

It all sounds very complicated and, in fact, it is. You'd have to be a chemist, nutritionist and full-time cook to turn out the kind of balanced diet that a puppy needs. Fortunately, all this hard work has been done for you. Nowhere is the increase in convenience foods more dramatic than in pet foods. The millions of research hours and dollars that have been devoted to the study of canine nutrition by such major manufacturers as Carnation Company have resulted in excellent prepared foods, scientifically balanced to provide all of a dog's nutrition needs. And for puppies, there are special foods that contain the extra vitamins and minerals he needs during the fast-growing months.

You'd do best to stick with the foods prepared by the experts. Don't take the risky route of trying to guess about your pet's diet. If you choose a commercial food of high quality, you can be sure puppy is getting all the nutrients he needs. And after all, the dog, too, is what he eats.

THE BILL OF FARE

Come 'N Get It is the latest product resulting from over 50 years of scientific study in canine nutrition at Friskies Research Kennels in Carnation, Washington, and at Carnation Nutritional Research Laboratories in Van Nuys, California. Carefully formulated to support growth and good health in puppies, it contains all the vitamins and minerals that are vital during the first year.

A dry food, Come 'N Get It contains 21 percent protein, more than the minimum requirement for growing pups. All you have to do is add warm water, milk or broth to bring out the aroma

and flavor and to give it the right consistency.
Mix the formula at a ratio of 1 cup of liquid to 2
cups of Come 'N Get It.

The chart below gives recommended amounts
of daily food intake, based on the dog's weight.
Since the amounts given are for dry food, the
bulk will increase somewhat with the addition of
liquid. And remember that these recommended
quantities are for *daily* servings, to be divided
into two, three or four meals, depending on the
age of the dog.

Puppy's Weight	Daily Amt. of Come 'N Get It	Puppy's Weight	Daily Amt. of Come 'N Get It
3-5 lbs.	1 cup	30-35 lbs.	7-8 cups
5-8 lbs.	1-2 cups	35-40 lbs.	8-9 cups
8-10 lbs.	2-3 cups	40-45 lbs.	9-10 cups
10-15 lbs.	3-4 cups	45-50 lbs.	10-11 cups
15-20 lbs.	4-5 cups	50-55 lbs.	11-12 cups
20-25 lbs.	5-6 cups	55-60 lbs.	12-13 cups
25-30 lbs.	6-7 cups		

*Divided into the number of daily feedings, as
required by the age of the dog.*

Come 'N Get It is by far the best basic diet
for your pet during his first year. From that
age on you can start introducing other foods to
accustom him to the diet that will be his adult
fare. Here are some guides. to selecting prepared
foods:

Dog foods fall into three general types. Learn
to read the labels. You will find some foods de-
scribed as "complete for both growth and mainte-
nance, "balanced" or "fully nourishing." These

are not idle boasts. Such claims are carefully regulated by state and federal agencies and mean that these foods meet nutritive requirements for a balanced diet. Some pet foods (such as some canned meats, chicken and fish) are meant only as supplements to add taste variety to the basic diet. A third kind of pet fare is the enormous selection of dog cookies, candies and other treats.

Supplements and snacks are fine for occasional treats, but not for a regular diet. Choose the foods labeled "complete" or "balanced." These come in both canned and dry forms. A few broken up chunks of canned Mighty Dog added to Come 'N Get It is a good way to introduce new tastes. Then gradually start giving your pet an occasional full meal of canned food. This will be a special treat, because dogs love the rich, meaty texture of canned Mighty Dog, and he'll soon let you know which of its flavors are his favorites.

Don't forget water! A dog's total body weight consists of 70 percent liquid, so water is absolutely essential to his health and comfort. Serve him fresh cool water along with his meals, and make it available to him, both indoors and outdoors, and at all times.

GOOD HABITS
Good eating habits are important, and now is the time to establish them. Here are some rules of puppy table etiquette; start them now and they'll become life-long patterns:
- Choose a quiet place for puppy's food and water bowls, and feed him there at regular times. Dogs like routine.

- Don't talk to him, tease or distract him in any way while he's eating.
- Give him 15 to 20 minutes to finish his meal, then remove the dish. If there is food left, reduce his rations at next mealtime. If he bolts his foods (most dogs are bolters) and noses around for more, try slightly larger servings.
- Don't feed him when he's excited or exhausted from play; give him a little water and let him rest before eating. Give him time to digest after meals, too—no playtime, car rides or excitement for at least an hour.
- Don't feed him between-meal treats. The only exceptions to this rule are rewards at the end of training sessions or for exceptionally good behavior. Nothing can lead to finicky food habits, overweight and even malnutrition as quickly as constant snacking between regular meals.
- Never offer him food from your own table. There are no exceptions to this rule. Puppy has a right to eat his dinner in peace and quiet, and so do you.

HOME COOKING

Variety in diet is not really important to a puppy. In fact, you should use restraint in adding special treats, because you can easily upset the balance that is so important to his continued growth, vitality and good health.

Still, it's natural to want to indulge your pet, especially that appealing puppy, with a little home cooking now and then. Fine—but follow three rigid rules in adding extras to his basic diet:

- Serve them only at mealtime, or puppy will get finicky—and fat.
- Never let them amount to more than 20 percent of his daily food intake, or you'll upset his nutritional balance.
- Be highly selective in tidbits and table scraps, or you'll have a sick pup.

What foods are suitable for a puppy? All breeds of dogs have exactly the same nutritional needs. A Chihuahua needs protein, fats, carbohydrates, vitamins and minerals in balanced proportion just as a Great Dane does. Obviously the quantity required varies greatly. Here is a list of do's and don'ts in puppy feeding, but remember that dogs have different tastes, and your pet is an individualist. He'll soon let you know what food he likes, and what foods agree with him.

Meat is rich in the protein necessary for growth and body repair. Red muscle meats can safely be served either raw or cooked; pork and fish should *always* be cooked. Do not cut all the fat away from meats. Puppy needs fat in his diet, and it provides a concentrated source of the calories needed during the period of rapid growth.

Starches and cereals are excellent sources of carbohydrates. Potatoes and rice must be cooked; uncooked starches are hard to digest and may cause diarrhea. Cereals also must be cooked, or a large part of them will be passed through undigested.

Eggs, milk and cheese are valuable foods that provide protein and fats. Eggs must be cooked, because raw egg white interferes with the absorption of the B vitamin, biotin. Milk is a good source of protein, but it is not essential if puppy is being fed a high quality commercial food.

Cooked chopped vegetables are high in vitamins and minerals, but also so high in water content that it takes very large quantities to be of real value. They are fine as occasional food supplements, however, if your pup has a taste for them. Mash them with cooked cereal and chopped meat, and be sure to add some of the water the vegetables were cooked in.

Rich gravies and sweets are as bad for puppy as they are for you. So are highly seasoned or heavily salted foods; puppy can't digest them and, in fact, salt is often used as an emetic for dogs. Clear those cocktail canapes away after the party. If puppy gets a crack at them, he's apt to have something worse than a hangover.

Hot or cold foods can turn a pup's appetite off completely. Serve his Come 'N Get It at about room temperature. That's the way he likes it, and warm liquid will bring out the flavor and aroma.

Bones are taboo. Large shank or knuckle bones are exceptions, of course, but even these have more value as teething tools and playthings than as food. Ground up bones, as used in commercial foods, are good for him, but those poultry, chop and steak bones from your table can do serious damage to puppy's stomach and intestines.

WEIGHT WATCHING

Early in this chapter you were told that a puppy should have all the food he will eat.

However, too much food and too little exercise is a lethal combination for man and dog alike. It is true that puppies can eat a great deal during this period of rapid growth. But don't let him eat to the point of getting bloated. If you see a bulging midriff developing, cut down on his rations. Obesity is a common and serious health problem, especially in older dogs, so you should start being your pup's weight watcher while he's young.

Chapter 7

TO HIS VERY GOOD HEALTH
(Medical Care)

Like human infants, puppies have lower resistance to disease than adult animals. In fact, not so many years ago less than half of all dogs born ever reached maturity.

These days puppy's chances are very good indeed. Dogs are healthier and live longer now, thanks to skilled medical attention and nutritious, scientifically balanced diets. But there is one more necessary ingredient in this magic mix for a long life—tender loving care at home.

PUPPY'S DOCTOR

Step one in puppy's health program is to choose his doctor, the veterinarian. This highly skilled specialist in animal diseases will be your invaluable ally throughout your pet's lifetime. Get to know him and to depend on him when your dog is ill or injured. Keep his address and telephone number (including his special night number, if he has one) in a prominent place where it will be available in emergencies. And make it a routine to have your pet examined twice yearly as his best possible health insurance.

Puppy should have his first checkup shortly after you adopt him. If he had a complete physical at the kennel, take that health record along on the first visit to your own veterinarian. He will then know what shots have been given and can schedule inoculations that are absolute musts to protect your pet against the four most lethal canine diseases:

- *Canine Parvovirus (CPV),* an extremely contagious disease that first appeared in 1978 and now occurs worldwide. The most common symptoms are sudden loss of appetite, and depression, usually followed by vomiting and severe diarrhea leading to dehydration. Another form of CPV that occurs in puppies less than 3 months of age is inflammation of the heart (myocarditis). In either form the disease progresses very rapidly and can be lethal to puppies. Treatment is difficult, but CPV can be prevented by vaccination. Don't delay. Consult your veterinarian about immunization as soon as you get your puppy.

- *Distemper,* a highly contagious virus disease that attacks the dog's tissues. Puppies are especially susceptible. Adult vaccination shots usually begin at 9 to 12 weeks, but your doctor may recommend puppy shots for temporary protection. Annual booster shots are necessary.
- *Hepatitis,* an infectious virus that affects the liver and gastrointestinal tract and may spread to other organs of the body, Again, puppies are especially prone, but can be immunized with shots given in combination with distemper and leptospirosis inoculations when he is 9 to 12 weeks old.
- *Leptospirosis,* an infectious disease that attacks the kidneys and liver, with symptoms similar to those for hepatitis. Immunization shots are given along with those for distemper and hepatitis; annual booster shots are required.
- *Rabies,* a virus disease of the nervous system, which is transmitted in the saliva of a rabid animal. Once the scourge of the canine world, rabies is now rare among dogs, thanks to immunization, *which is required by law.* The disease has shown alarming increase among some wild animals in recent years, so it's still a threat, especially to the country dog. Don't be a putter-offer when it comes to rabies shots; you cannot get a license for your dog until you show proof of inoculation. Rabies shots are given at 4 to 6 months, followed by boosters at annual or 30-month intervals, depending on the type of vaccine used by your veterinarian.

Many veterinarians keep records of shots needed and send out reminder cards to their clients. It might be a good idea to inquire whether your doctor provides this service. If not, keep your own records as self-reminders.

BEAUTY TREATMENT

During the first visit, the veterinarian will take care of any grooming needs that were not handled by the breeder. If you bought from a kennel, puppy's dewclaws (a residual thumb just above the paws) may already have been removed. The same is true of tail docking. Both of these operations, show requirements for some breeds, are best performed a few days after birth. If the kennel did not handle these, consult your veterinarian on the advisability of performing them on your particular pet.

Ask your doctor to give you a nail-trimming demonstration. This is a part of grooming (see Chapter 9) that is easy to handle at home, once you know how. Adult dogs usually get enough exercise to keep their nails worn down, but puppies, who spend a lot of time indoors, sometimes need your help. Overly long nails can cause pain, spreading of the toes or splaying of the feet and, in some cases, even lameness.

GOOD HEALTH—AND BAD

Puppies are easy marks for all ailments, from bee stings to belly aches, that easily beset the young. Most of his troubles will be minor ones, to be treated with tenderness and common sense. But you should be able to recognize the symptoms of genuine illness, so that you can alert your doctor.

Very generally, a sick dog will have what veterinarians and breeders call an "unthrifty" appearance. A scruffy coat, dull eyes, poor appetite and general lethargy are signs of trouble. So, especially for puppies, are runny eyes or nose or an abnormally bloated stomach. Persistent constipation, diarrhea or vomiting are also danger signals.

Persistent is the key word, however. A puppy can seem "sick as a dog" one moment and come bounding back, bigger than life, the next. Give him time for his own recuperative powers to work. See that he gets lots of rest and, above all, keep him warm. Drafts and chills can cause serious complications if he does have an infection. If he's not bouncy and bright-eyed within 24 hours, call the doctor. Here are some of the things to watch for if your pup seems under par:

Vomiting is not necessarily serious. Dogs can regurgitate at will, and this may be puppy's way— or his stomach's—of rejecting something he has eaten. Chewing grass, overeating, any number of things can cause him to vomit. If he seems relieved and comfortable after he upchucks, there's probably nothing to worry about. If it continues, vomiting could be an indication of worms or other parasites, a foreign object lodged in his throat or stomach, or the onset of a disease. Take him off food and liquids for 24 hours, but let him lick ice cubes occasionally. If he seems weak and sickly, take his temperature. If he has a fever, or if there is blood in the vomit, get professional help immediately.

Diarrhea is another common complaint that is not serious unless it continues for longer than 24 hours, or recurs very frequently, or is accompanied by fever. It usually indicates nothing more than a mild stomach upset. Withhold food and liquids for 24 hours (but offer ice cubes) and feed him Kaopectate or Pepto Bismol every two hours. Quantities vary according to size of the dog. A tablespoon per dosage is about right for a 20-pound dog, less for a smaller animal. After 24 hours, start feeding him starchy foods such as cooked rice, macaroni or potatoes until the condition has cleared up. Persistent diarrhea or either blood or mucus in the stools are serious symptoms and call for professional treatment. Constipation occurs less frequently in young dogs than among older animals. In puppies, it can result from poor diet or an intestinal obstruction caused by a foreign object the dog has swallowed. Milk of Magnesia, one teaspoon per every 10 pounds of dog, is a safe and effective laxative. *Do not experiment with human laxatives;* some of them contain strychnine which, even in minute quantities, is lethal to dogs. If you suspect that your pup has swallowed something that is causing an obstruction, don't give laxatives at all, but call the veterinarian immediately.

Convulsions are a symptom, not a disease. They may be caused by a serious ailment, such as distemper or epilepsy, or by something as common to puppyhood as teething, worms, a foreign object in the stomach or intestines, indigestion, or even extreme heat. A fit is frightening to watch, and there isn't much you can do except try to protect your pet from injuring himself. Throw a towel, coat or blanket over him and hold him gently until the seizure subsides. Then comfort him (he's frightened, too), keep him warm and quiet, and get in touch with your veterinarian for a diagnosis of the cause.

Coughing and a runny nose can mean a respiratory infection or the approach of a whole range of serious diseases. If they are accompanied by a fever, call your doctor at once. If not, they probably indicate a mild upper respiratory infection that will clear up within a few days. Keep puppy indoors and out of drafts until the symptoms disappear. Lots of sleep and a little sympathy are indicated.

A persistent, hacking, dry cough may signal infectious tracheobronchitis, or kennel cough. This is an extremely contagious disease that spreads rapidly among animals closely confined in the same quarters. For this reason, a puppy should not be boarded or hospitalized unless absolutely necessary or unless he can be isolated. Kennel cough is a mild, but stubborn, disease that can hang on for as long as two to three weeks. Keep your dog warm and quiet, and put him under a doctor's care. If not treated, kennel cough may lead to serious complications.

TEETHING

Most puppies lose their milk teeth at around four or five months (don't worry if he swallows them; they're soft), and acquire a full set of permanent ones by the sixth month. The whole process takes place so fast that it sometimes causes diarrhea, listlessness, poor appetite, weight loss and even a little fever. In rare cases, teething has been known to bring on convulsions. Most often, however, the symptoms are nothing more severe than a slightly cranky pup and sudden increase of teeth marks on every chewable object in the house. Give him sympathy—and something tough to chew on.

Puppy will get 42 permanent teeth in all, and if he is getting a balanced diet of fortified puppy food, his teeth will come in straight and strong. It's not a bad idea to have your veterinarian give him a mouth check at teething time, possibly when you take him in for inoculations.

THE PARASITES

Worms are internal parasites that plague many dogs—perhaps most—at some time during their lives. Puppies are their special prey. The type of worm that most commonly infests the young dog is the roundworm, sometimes called "puppy worm." An infestation is not difficult to control, unless it is allowed to progress too far. You may actually see worms in your pet's vomit or feces, but any of the following signs could indicate their presence:

- The dog seems weak and listless.
- His appetite changes; he may frantically stuff himself or completely ignore his food.

- He has loose bowel movements which may be flecked with blood.
- He develops a scruffy coat and generally un-thrifty appearance.
- He may lose weight or develop an abnormal-ly distended stomach.

These are signs that something's wrong, and it may or may not be worms. The only way you can be sure is to take a sample of your dog's stool to the veterinarian. Don't give puppy patent worm-ing medicines "just in case." Deworming can be successfully done at home, but only under your veterinarian's direction and using drugs pre-scribed by him. Home cures, if administered in an inexpert and careless way, can do as much harm as the infestation itself.

Beware of homespun advice about worms; the subject is loaded with old wives' tales. You'll be told that when a dog scoots along on the floor on his rear, it's a sure sign he has worms. Not necessarily. Worms might possibly cause this, but scooting is usually a sign that the anal sacs or glands are irritated or impacted. One of the most durable myths is that milk and sweets cause worms. Not true. A puppy can be born with worms, or get them by swallowing the eggs which hatch in the intestines. Someone will surely rec-commend that age-old home cure for worms, gar-lic. Not true. Garlic may smell strong enough to be a dewormer, but only medicine prescribed by your veterinarian will rid puppy of these parasites.

External parasites such as fleas and ticks are far more than nuisances, though they are most decidedly that. They are disease carriers, too. For a description of the most common skin pests, their prevention and control, see Chapter 9.

HOME NURSING

Except in extreme cases, home is the place for the sick pup. He's happier there, and he won't be exposed to other ailing animals. For this reason, you should know a few rules of home nursing.

To take his temperature, use a rectal thermometer coated with Vaseline or K-Y lubricant, which is water soluble. Insert the thermometer halfway, and hold for two minutes. (It may take two people for this job.) Normal temperature is 101 to 102. Do *not* rely on the cold-nose myth as a health barometer. It is not an accurate one. A dog's nose can be warm and dry simply from his sleeping in a warm and dry room.

To give him medicine, try burying it in his favorite food or a special treat. Puppies are such gobblers that this will probably work, but if he eats his way around it, here is what you must do:

- For pills, grasp his muzzle and squeeze the lips against his teeth to force his mouth open, then tilt his head backward and place (don't throw) the pill as far back as you can push it. Hold his mouth closed and massage his throat for a moment to make him swallow. A little butter on the pill will help it slide down more easily.
- For liquids, pull puppy's cheek out to make a lip pouch, pour the medicine in slowly, then close the pouch and let him swallow.

To give an enema, use an adult or infant-sized rectal syringe, depending on the size of the dog, and coat the tip of the nozzle with Vaseline or mineral oil for lubrication. Put him in the bathtub or outdoors, and you'd better have someone around to help, because he's not going to like this. Insert the nozzle gently and hold the bag a foot or two above his head, raising and lowering it so that the water will not flow with too much pressure. There are also disposable plastic squeeze bottles, called Fleet Enemas, that are convenient and easy to use. These come in various sizes to suit your breed. Consult your doctor before you give puppy an enema; in most cases a mild laxative will do the job, and with less trauma for both you and your pet.

TRAVEL TIPS

What does travel have to do with good health? In puppy's case, everything. The puppy under six months of age should stay home. He hasn't the resistance to withstand exposure to other animals in a boarding kennel. And he certainly hasn't the manners yet to make him a welcome guest anywhere.

Still, people travel—so what to do about puppy? If possible, hire a sitter; if that is not possible, select a boarding kennel that provides special care for puppies. Many veterinary clinics that also board dogs will not accept puppies because of the danger of exposure. But with a little careful shopping, you should be able to find a kennel that will provide protection from contagion and give him attention and care. Be sure your pup gets all needed vaccinations at least 7 days prior to boarding.

Chapter 8

IN CASE OF ACCIDENT...
(First Aid for Puppies)

A puppy will try anything. He pokes his nose and his paws into everything from paint to pesticides. He chews and swallows whatever he can get into his mouth. He runs headlong and unheeding to greet you, even if you're across the street. He thinks the world is his oyster, he's rarin' to go, he's a daredevil. And sometimes he gets into trouble.

You'll have to watch him carefully until he picks up a little common dog sense. You should also know the fundamentals of first aid, so that you can soothe the big and little hurts of puppy-hood. In extreme cases, first aid might even save your pup's life.

FIRST AID FOR PUPPIES

In serious accidents, the basic rules of first aid for humans apply to dogs, too:

- Do not move the injured victim.
- Stop excessive bleeding immediately.
- Keep him warm and quiet in case of shock.
- Do not give liquids, in case of internal in-juries.

Restraint. A puppy in pain may panic and have to be restrained from biting while you treat his injury. If there's no one around to help, muzzle him with a mouth tie. To do this, take a strip of cloth (or a necktie, stocking, whatever is handy) and loop it over his nose, making sure the nostrils are free. Tie it under his chin, then run the ends under his ears and tie them behind his head. Make sure the tie doesn't obstruct his breathing, and remove it immediately if he seems to be gagging or trying to vomit.

Shock. This is a critical condition that results, usually, from very serious injuries, but in rare cases even from extreme fright. The symptoms are a cold body, feeble pulse, shallow breathing and prostration. There's no time for delay; shock is extremely dangerous. Cover your pet with blankets and put a hot water bottle or a heating pad next to him to raise his body temperature. Keep him very quiet and call the doctor at once. Try reviving him with a sniff of aromatic spirits of ammonia, if available. Do *not* force liquids; there may be internal injuries.

External Bleeding. Shallow bleeding is not serious. Profuse bleeding may mean a punctured artery and must be stopped. The quickest and by far the most effective method is simply to apply pressure directly to the wound and hold firmly until help arrives. The tourniquet is also effective, assuming that the injury is in a location where this is practical. Just be sure to apply the tourniquet *above the wound* and toward the heart, and remember to loosen it every ten minutes or so for circulation.

Artificial Respiration. If your dog seems to have stopped breathing but you can feel a heartbeat (a condition that might be brought on by electric shock or by suffocation, for example), try to revive him with artificial respiration. Mouth-to-mouth resuscitation, applied by cupping the hands and breathing directly into the dog's mouth and nose, is the most effective (but also most difficult to apply). The other method is to place puppy on his side, head and neck extended and his tongue pulled forward. Press firmly on his ribs, behind the shoulder blade, to force air out of the lungs. Relax immediately, count to five, and then press again. Repeat these movements, smoothly and rhythmically, until the dog begins to breathe. When he revives, treat him for shock.

Fractures. The symptoms of broken bones or dislocations are clear; you'll know simply by the way puppy walks or holds his damaged limb. Fractures call for professional care, of course, but be sure to keep him very quiet to prevent further injury until you can get him to the doctor. If he's too big and active to restrain, you may have to immobilize the area with a temporary splint firmly bandaged to the limb, but not so tight as to impair circulation.

Poisoning. Pain, drooling, trembling, vomiting, panting and convulsions are all possible signs of poisoning. They are also symptoms of many other canine maladies, but in the case of poison are apt to be more severe. It is important to act quickly; any delay can be fatal. First, immediately give puppy an emetic of equal parts hydrogen peroxide (medicinal, not hair bleach) and warm water. A tablespoon of mustard powder mixed with water, or a strong salt water (2 teaspoons to a cup) are also effective emetics. Follow this with an antidote of activated charcoal, 3 tablespoons mixed in a cup of warm water. If this is not available, give him a mixture of egg white and milk. *Call your veterinarian immediately;* poisons can take effect very rapidly.

Burns. Apply burn medicine from an aerosol spray or tannic acid jelly or concentrated cool tea to heat burns. Burns caused by chemicals such as acids should be washed with a solution of baking or washing soda, 1 tablespoon to a pint of warm water, then treated as heat burns. Small, super-

ficial burns can be soothed by applying ice cubes
or cold water, then burn ointment.

Bee or Wasp Stings. Apply a cold compress to relieve pain, then cover with a pain-killing ointment,
or with a heavy paste of bicarbonate of soda or
plain starch. Dogs sometimes go into shock as a
result of bee or wasp stings. Follow the directions
for shock treatment and call your veterinarian.

Foreign Objects Swallowed. This is the kind of
accident that puppies specialize in; they seem to
learn about life by chewing a path through it. A
young Basset hound named Annabelle had to go
into surgery because of severe stomach pains and
a tendency to rattle when she walked. It seems
that Annabelle had swallowed six marbles, a half-
dozen rocks and two rubber balls. A six-month-
old German Shepherd chose a diet even more bi-
zarre. Her operation yielded 15 pins, a buckle, a
ball, several strips of leather, and the tassel from
a pin cushion.

Veterinarians' files are full of such abdominal
inventories. The dog's stomach is a tough organ
that can digest or pass on some incredible objects.
But there are things that can do serious damage
to a puppy's insides. Your best course is to make
your house and yard as puppy-proof as possible
by putting all swallowable objects out of reach.
Be especially eagle-eyed for the following:
- Sharp things that can tear or puncture, such
  as pins, needles, children's jacks or beer-can
  and soft-drink tabs.
- Objects that splinter easily, such as glass and
  wooden or plastic toys.

- All small bones. These are lethal. Poultry bones splinter into dagger-sharp pieces; chewed chop and steak bones can become impacted in the stomach. *Only* large, hard bones such as a shank or knuckle are safe.
- Anything made of soft rubber, such as many children's playthings. Soft rubber tears easily and can stick to puppy's insides, blocking the intestinal tract. Hard or simulated rubber toys are safe if they're large enough; keep him away from objects he can swallow in one piece.
- Painted toys. Puppy might get a toxic dose of lead paint.
- Poisons. These are the most dangerous of all, and they lurk in surprising and unsuspected places. Human medicines and cosmetics, deodorant soaps, household cleaning agents, aerosol sprays, garden sprays, garden insecticides, snail and rodent poisons—all can be toxic to a dog. High shelves and locked cabinets are the best insurance.

Puppy will eventually outgrow his chewing habits. Until he does, confine him to one pup-safe area when you're not around to keep an eye on him. Give him some tough playthings of his own, such as hard or simulated rubber toys, strips of rawhide, or even an old leather shoe (but lock your closet; he can't tell old from new). A shank or knucklebone will give him a good workout, but take it away if it starts softening. Give him lots of companionship and play time; excessive chewing is sometimes a symptom of loneliness.

If, in spite of all precautions, you see your pet gulping, gagging or pawing repeatedly at his muzzle, it is probably a sign that something is lodged in his mouth or throat. Force his mouth open by pressing the thumb and forefinger of one hand on both sides of his cheeks. Examine his mouth carefully to see if something is lodged in his throat or between his teeth, and if it not too deeply embedded, pull it out with your fingers or long-nosed pliers. Caution is the rule here, however. If there is danger of the object breaking or becoming even more deeply lodged, get professional help immediately.

When you know your pup has swallowed something that might cause trouble, you can force him to vomit by giving an emetic. This is effective only if given shortly after ingestion, and should not be used if something sharp, like a needle, has made its way down. If puppy shows continued signs of distress—pawing at his mouth, vomiting, a sore and distended stomach—get him to a veterinarian quickly.

Electric Shock. Puppies sometimes chew far enough into electric light cords to suffer mouth burns or even shock. If this happens, *do not touch your pet until you have pulled out the plug*. Revive him with a whiff of ammonia, followed by strong coffee or a little whiskey in water. If his mouth is burned, treat it with strong tea. Keep light cords unplugged when puppy is alone in the house.

Heatstroke. The symptoms are loud, continuous

panting, difficulty in breathing, extreme weakness and, in some cases, unconsciousness. Heatstroke is an extremely critical condition, because the dog may go into shock. Call your veterinarian at once, but until he arrives, cool puppy off as quickly as possible. Place him in a cool, shady spot and sponge him down gently with cold water. Use smelling salts, if they're handy, and when he revives give him a little black coffee. Keep him quiet and see that he gets lots of rest for the next few days. Ice packs and cold-water enemas, often recommended for the older dog suffering from heatstroke, are not for puppies. Either treatment might bring on shock or a case of pneumonia in the young dog.

One of the most common causes of canine heatstroke, and a tragically common cause of death, is leaving dogs in closed cars during hot weather. The temperature inside an automobile can reach as high as 120 degrees on a hot day. Anyone who leaves a puppy in a closed car is only asking for trouble, such as a few holes chewed in the upholstery. But if you must (and you're sure that puppy won't panic), lock the car and lower all the windows a few inches for ventilation, but not far enough for him to escape. Park in the shade, but remember that the sun shifts position, so don't be gone for longer than 15 minutes. Better leave a water bowl too, if it's a hot day. Dogs can't take much heat.

FIRST AID KIT
When an animal is injured, you won't have time to rummage around in a frantic search for some-

thing to help him. First aid has to be right away. For this reason it's a very good idea to set aside a box containing puppy's own medicines and the equipment you will need in case of emergency. His medicine chest should include the following:

- Adhesive tape and bandages for dressing wounds.
- Antiseptics, such as Merthiolate, Metaphen or peroxide for cleansing wounds, and Neosporin ointment to prevent infection.
- Burn medicines contained in aerosol sprays, as prescribed by your veterinarian.
- Aromatic spirits of ammonia for shock treatment.
- Hydrogen peroxide, mustard powder or salt for emetics.
- Activated charcoal as a poison antidote.
- Milk of magnesia to serve as a laxative.
- Kaopectate or milk of bismuth to control diarrhea.
- A rectal thermometer and Vaseline or K-Y lubricant.
- Blunt-ended scissors for cutting hair away from wounds.

SAFETY FIRST

Most accidents, after all, are the result of neglect. By far the greatest cause of serious injury and death in dogs, for example, is the automobile. It takes only one moment of neglect, one moment off the leash or out of the fenced yard, to cause this tragedy.

An ounce of prevention will work its proverbial magic if you will only observe a few simple safety

rules for your pup. Here, then, are some guidelines
for accident prevention:

Keep your dog confined when he's outdoors. If
your yard is fenced, make sure there are no holes
he can wriggle through, that the gate latches firmly and that family and visitors are warned to close
it securely. If the yard is not fenced, then you
should construct some kind of run or play area
for puppy. It need not be large; even a playpen,
placed in a shady spot in the garden, will work
as a temporary measure. Put in a weighted pan
of water and a few toys to amuse puppy when he's
alone.

For a permanent run, enclose an area with
sturdy metal fencing at least 6 feet high (dogs
are amazingly adept at climbing). A run 6 feet
wide and 20 to 30 feet long is large enough for
almost all breeds. Cover the surface with a porous
material, such as sand or gravel; plain earth holds
the dampness and is unsanitary. Choose a location
that provides both sun and shade, keep the run
clean and always provide water. Make sure there
are no garden poisons or pesticides within puppy's
reach. Clear the yard of broken glass, stones,
small pebbles, or any other objects that he might
swallow.

Never unleash puppy when you are walking
him on a public street. In one unleashed instant
he might dash into the path of an oncoming car.
If he rides in the car with you, always attach his
leash to his collar before you open the door; he
might bolt head-on into the traffic.

Keep puppy confined to his crate or playpen
when he's alone in the house. If he's getting too

old for this kind of treatment, put him in a room that has been carefully puppy-proofed: light cords disconnected, all swallowable objects removed, nothing to chew on but his own safe toys. And keep an eye on him when he has the run of the house. Make sure all household poisons such as cleaning agents and human medicines are out of reach. He's not actually looking for trouble, but he does have a way of finding it.

Chapter 9

SKIN DEEP
(Grooming and Skin Care)

To many dog owners the word "grooming" means pompom haircuts, beribboned bangs, and doggy perfumes. Fine for little Fifi, they say, but not for Andy. He's all dog, he is.

But Andy needs it, too. Grooming is not just a matter of good looks, though that certainly is a side benefit. A better word for it would be cleanliness. The few minutes a day it takes to comb and brush puppy's coat will pay enormous dividends in his health and well-being. He'll be less prone to parasites and skin ailments. He will look bet-

ter, feel better and hold his head a little higher.
There's a bonus in it for you, too. Your house will
be cleaner.

As with all good habits, the time to start is
while your pet is young. Don't expect too much
of him in the beginning. He may try to play tug-
of-war with the grooming comb, or roll over to
have his belly scratched, or simply try to bolt for
the blue. Keep at it; all dogs like to be fondled,
and puppies fairly dote on it. In time he'll enjoy
his grooming sessions.

HOW TO GROOM

The equipment for grooming is simple. The basic
tool is a wire slicker brush, to remove loose hairs
and work out snarls. For a long-haired dog you
will also need a comb with widely spaced, blunt
teeth and a brush with long, stiff bristles; for a
short-haired dog, a short-bristled brush or hound
glove (a mitt made for grooming). For wire-haired
breeds you should have a stripping knife. You will
also need barber scissors and dog's nail clippers.
All of these are available at pet supply stores.

Place puppy on a table or bench to groom him.
This will not only make it easier for you to work,
it will make it clear to him that this is business,
not some new form of play. At Friskies Research
Kennels, table training is started with each individual member of a litter as early as four or five
weeks of age, and we have found that these brief
sessions establish an important social bond between puppy and his handler.

But you must, of course, be very gentle and reassuring. Talk to puppy, pet him and praise him

as you work rapidly. First go over his coat with a wire slicker brush to remove loose hairs and snarls. Follow this with a combing, then give him a good brushing to make his coat shine. The brush alone will usually do the job for short-haired dogs, but do not neglect their grooming; some of the short-coated breeds are among the heaviest shedders of all.

When your wire-haired or long-haired dog is shedding heavily, you should run a stripping knife through his coat frequently to remove excess hair. In fact, all wire-haired breeds should be completely stripped at least twice a year. This will help keep him cool during hot weather too, but don't clip your dog too short in the summertime. It only makes him itchy, uncomfortable, and easy prey to sunburn.

THE PEDICURE
You should trim puppy's nails occasionally. If a dog's nails grow too long, they can cause his foot to splay or spread, making it difficult for him to walk. It's a good idea to have your veterinarian demonstrate nail clipping the first time, and don't attempt the job yourself until puppy is thoroughly accustomed to his grooming sessions.

Some dogs hate to have their nails clipped. Be very gentle and reassuring, and work for brief periods at a time. Use clippers made for animals, and cut only the tip, or transparent part, of the nail. Be careful not to cut into the quick, because this can cause pain and bleeding. The quick is apparent in clear nails, but not in black ones; to be safe, clip only a little at a time. Don't forget

the dewclaws, if they have not been removed.
These vestigial toes have nails which, if not
trimmed, may curve back into the flesh.

THE BATH

If you groom your pet daily or even several
times a week, he should rarely need a bath. In
fact, dogs under six months of age should not be
bathed at all. Puppies are highly susceptible to
respiratory infections, and there is simply too
much danger of chills. If your pup gets very dirty,
give him a warm water sponge bath, followed by
a rubdown with a turkish towel. There are also
dry shampoos on the market that do a satisfactory
job. Fuller's earth or plain cornmeal rubbed into
his coat are also good cleaning agents. Brush
them out thoroughly, and then rub him down with
a cloth dampened in warm water.

Even the older pup should be bathed infre-
quently. Dogs do not perspire through their skin,
so the dirt on their coats is external and super-
ficial. But every now and then an adolescent pup
gets into trouble that only soap and water can
cure. When that happens, roll up your sleeves and
make it as painless as possible. Puppy's first bath
mustn't frighten him, or he may be tub shy for
the rest of his life.

The most important precautions are to protect
his eyes and ears. Put a little Vaseline or a few
drops of eye ointment (mineral oil will do, too) in
the corner of each eye to form a protective film.
And be very careful to keep soap and water away
from his ears, which are extremely sensitive and
prone to infection. Never wash them with water;

if they need cleaning, gently swab them with cotton dipped in mineral oil.

Bathe puppy in a well-heated, draft-free room. Use warm water (give it the elbow test; remember that dogs are very sensitive to heat) with a mild soap or shampoo that will work up a good lather. Rinse very thoroughly, because soap can be irritating to the skin. Get him as close to dry as possible by rubbing him with coarse towels, and then keep him inside for an hour or two. This will keep him out of drafts, and also out of the nearest mud puddle or dirt pile—his sure-fire target if he escapes your clutches.

EXTERNAL PARASITES

While you're grooming puppy, keep an eye out for skin parasites. Regular combing or brushing will go a long way on the anti-itch battle, but it is also important to keep his living quarters clean. Give his bed or kennel a good scrubbing and airing occasionally, and spray them with an insecticide. This attacks the critter's breeding ground. Here are the most common skin pests:

- *Fleas* hop around on a dog's body to do their biting, so it takes only a few to make him miserable and to start a flea colony. Don't wait until puppy is miserable from itching to wage war. Groom him regularly, and at the first sign of an invasion use an insecticide spray or powder, as recommended by you veterinarian. *Be sure the insecticide is labeled safe for dogs*, and don't forget to spray his sleeping quarters, too. Flea collars are not recommended for puppies. The collars contain pesticides that are fatal to fleas, but might cause skin irritations and even illness in the young dog.

- *Ticks* are tenacious little bloodsuckers that bury their heads under a dog's skin. They used to be strictly country pests, but now they are widely prevalent in cities, too, especially in the summer. Female ticks are the vampires. When imbedded they look like warts or flat blackish-brown seeds which become swollen when filled with blood. While grooming puppy, run your hands carefully over his body. If you find a tick, first saturate it with alcohol, then grasp it close to the dog's skin with tweezers and pull it out very carefully. Make sure no part of the imbedded head remains to cause an infection. Spray puppy's living quarters.

- *Mites* are too small to see, but the signs of infestation are the same as for other pests—frantic scratching, or biting and chewing at the coat. Mites are the most dangerous of all the skin pests, because they introduce the unpleasant and serious skin disease, mange. Danger signs to watch for are small skin lesions, scabs, itching, inflammation, thickening of the skin, or extreme shedding of hair. One variety, otodectic mange, affects the dog's ears; symptoms are ear discharge, carrying the head at a strange angle, scratching, or shaking the head. Mange is difficult to treat and impossible for the amateur to diagnose. The key to cure is early treatment.

Don't delay if your dog has a puzzling skin irritation. Get him to the veterinarian.

THE DANDIES

The quick comb-and-brush treatment is common garden variety grooming, designed to keep puppy's coat clean and healthy. But there are some breeds that take more time and skill—and in some cases, professional help—in their beauty treatments. Any self-respecting Pomeranian, Pekingese, Lhasa Apso or Shih Tzu will expect to have his handsome fur brushed and brushed and *brushed*. The Yorkshire Terrier spends half his time having his long, silky coat primped to perfection. Some of the wire-haired terriers have a much more spit-and-polish appearance if they get an occasional professional trim. And there's always the Poodle! He can be clipped in as many styles as a topiary garden.

But the dog beauty parlor is not for puppy—not quite yet. Meanwhile, get him used to the comb and brush. Even if he does turn to the professional later on, he'll always need home grooming. Because even the dandiest dogs get dirty.

Chapter 10

GOOD MANNERS
(Obedience Training for the Older Pup)

By the time he is six months old, puppy has learned the rudiments of good behavior. He's been housebroken for some time. He's learned, let us hope, that it's against the rules to jump up on beds, sofas, chairs or people. He responds—well, most of the time—to such words as "no," "come," "down" and "quiet." He knows what "good dog" and "bad dog" mean, and he's a little bit of both.

Now, at somewhere between 6 and 9 months, it's time for puppy to progress into regular obedience training. Don't skip this part of your pet's education. It's not difficult; a daily 10-minute session will work wonders. Dogs like to be trained, and your work sessions will even further strengthen the bond between you. A well-trained dog is a source of great pride and joy. And most important of all, obedience training is essential to your dog's own safety.

You can go as far as you want with this. Dogs can be trained to do almost anything. They will speak, beg, roll over and play dead for the doubtful amusement of your friends. They will serve as seeing eyes for the blind and hearing ears for the deaf. They will guard children, track down fugitives, and fight in wars.

But parlor tricks and working careers have little to do with regular obedience training. What is essential is that your dog learn to obey the following basic commands: sit, heel, stay and come. These are not for show. These are to keep him safe.

GOING TO SCHOOL

Obedience classes for canines are available in almost every community now. They range from self-governed clubs of pet owners who simply enjoy working together to highly professional schools that train dogs for show. Their prices range accordingly. In some areas there are free obedience classes operated by the local SPCA or humane society.

Professional obedience schools offer the advantage of training you to train your dog. The leaders will be as quick to spot your mistakes as puppy's.

and just as strict in correcting them. Also, dogs do learn from each other. In a highly disciplined class atmosphere, even a frisky puppy will follow the example set by other dogs—for a while, at least. You must remember that young dogs have a short attention span. Most obedience classes will not accept a dog under six months of age, and some not under one year.

If you have a purebred pup that you plan to enter in shows, then a professional school would be a good investment for you. If you have a problem pup, take him to a professional trainer; your dog will get expert and individual training. Or if you simply enjoy working with other pet owners, then by all means enroll in a class. Your veterinarian or local humane organization will refer you to training schools in your area.

HOME TUTORING

The basic obedience commands can also be taught at home, and there are strong arguments for home training. Whether you choose a class or the do-it-yourself method, you will have to work with puppy, at home, every day. And after all, home is where the obedience action is. You want puppy to "stay" in his own backyard, to "sit" in his own living room when guests arrive, to "come" when he decides to pursue a passing bicycle. So why not teach him on home grounds?

Anyone in the family can be puppy's trainer, but it should always be the same person. Training is a one-to-one thing; a dog learns as much from consistent voice inflections and body movements as from word commands. Children make fine trainers, but they must be willing to set aside at least 10 minutes *every day* to work patiently with their pet.

RULES FOR THE TRAINER
And whoever does the job must first teach himself some simple rules of human etiquette in dealing with dogs. Your pup wants to learn; you'll have no trouble if you follow these guidelines:

Reward and punishment are the bases for all training. For a reward, praise and a loving caress are all that a dog asks. The experienced handlers at Friskies Research Kennels advise against food tidbits; they're apt to distract puppy from his work. Your approval is what puppy is working for, so praise—lavish, triumphant praise—is the magic ingredient of obedience training.

As for punishment, a sharp verbal reprimand is enough. Do not strike your puppy; it accomplishes nothing and may instill fear. If a sharper rebuke is called for, give a quick jerk at his collar or leash as you say "No!" Never harangue; get the correction over with quickly and move on. And always punish *only* at the moment of the crime; even a few seconds later he won't know what you're scolding him for.

Work for brief periods only. Puppies tire easily, and 10 to 15 minutes is as long as you can expect to hold his attention. Choose a time when he's rested and relaxed, not after play or just before meals.

Be consistent in your commands, body movements and voice inflections. Use the same words —simple, short words—to tell him what you want him to do. Repeat and repeat and *repeat*. Master one command completely before you move on to the next.

Tailor your teaching technique to match your dog's disposition. The shy and timid pup needs a great deal of praise and encouragement. The aggressive, high-strung animal calls for a stricter hand.

End every training session on a success. This has great psychological importance. Puppy has worked hard, even if not always effectively, and he needs your praise and approval.

TRAINING TOOLS
For equipment you will need a leather leash, 6 to 7 feet long, with a strong bolt-type snap on one end and a loop on the other. (Don't allow puppy to chew on his leash, and *never* strike him with it.) You will also need a slip collar, which is a chain with a ring on each end. Hold one of the rings in your fingers and drop the chain through it; this forms a loose-fitting chin noose to slip over puppy's head. *The slip collar is for training only*. Never let

puppy wear it when he's running free; it might get caught in something and choke him.

Always keep your dog on your left side during training. Hold the leash in your right hand, doubled up into a loop so that you have a short (but not tight) lead. The loop can be dropped to allow more slack in case puppy suddenly lunges forward. But the short lead is important for corrections. When your pup makes a mistake, snap or jerk the leash. This is puppy's reminder that he is to do as *you* say, not what *he* wants. Make the snap correction quick and sharp. Don't drag it out; this is a signal, not a punishment.

Keep your body movements consistent; these convey as much to the dog as word commands. Follow these rules:

- When you wish the dog to accompany you, always start with your left foot. Left foot first will become a recognized cue to walk.
- When you are going to leave the dog, start with your right foot. Right foot first becomes the signal to "stay."
- When you stop, always stop on the right foot and bring the left foot into place.

THE COMMANDS

"*Sit*" is the first, and one of the simplest, of the basic commands. Place puppy on your left side, his leash gathered in your right hand so that you have a grip fairly close to his collar. Say "Sit!" and at the same time push down on his hindquarters with your left hand while you pull up on the leash with your right. Pulling up on the leash will keep his head raised so that he can't lie down.

Hold your left hand pressure on his rump for a while, so that he doesn't jump up before the lesson is learned. Praise him.

Repeat this procedure many times. When you think he's getting the idea, discontinue the pressure on the rump and use only the leash as you say "Sit." When he's mastered that, use the command alone, still on leash but without the upward tug on it. And finally, when he's performed many times without error, take him off leash and say "Sit!" He should come at once to your left side and sit quietly. *Good dog!*

"Heel" immediately follows the "Sit" command; in fact, many trainers teach the two together. Place puppy in a sitting position at your left side, his leash gathered loosely in your right hand. Your left hand is free, but you will use it to give him signals on the leash. Now give the leash a quick snap with your left hand, say "Heel!" and step forward with your *left* foot. All these signals —the snap on the leash, the verbal command, and the step forward—must be given simultaneously. When puppy walks at your side in heel position, praise him profusely. When he goes too far forward, slow down a bit, snap back on the leash with your left hand and repeat the command "Heel!" When he lags behind, go through the same motions with a forward snap on the leash. He'll soon learn that the most comfortable spot for him is at your left side. Praise him.

In practicing heeling, stop and start frequently, using the "Sit" command at the end of each walk and the "Heel" command at the start. Remember always to start on the left foot. Keep the leash slack in your right hand, and touch it with your left hand only to make snap corrections. All these signals mean something to your dog. Practice over and over; reverse directions, turning sometimes to the right, sometimes to the left. Such maneuvers create more chances for error, but this is how puppy learns.

Practice has made him perfect? Then try this exercise, *on* leash, in the park or on busy streets, around people and other dogs. If he's really mastered "Heel" and "Sit," distractions won't interfere with his performance. *Good boy!*

"Stay" is a little more difficult. Puppy doesn't *want* to stay; he wants to be with you. Once again, place him in the sitting position on your left side, the leash hanging loosely in your right hand. Now say "Stay" in a quiet but commanding tone and, at the same time, place your left hand in front of his nose without touching it. Then step out, *right foot first*, in the direction you were facing. Take a few short steps and turn around to face your dog; if he stays for a few seconds, return to him by walking around his left side to your original position. Stand quietly for a moment, then praise him.

This is an exercise in control, so it's important to be calm and deliberate in voice and movements. If puppy follows you or lies down, quickly correct him with a sharp jerk on the leash and a "No!" You can expect him to move at first, but in time he'll get the idea. When this begins to happen, gradually increase the distance you move away from him until you're at the end of his leash.

Then further increase the distance by tying a piece of rope to the leash. In the advanced stages of this exercise you should be able to move into another room, leaving your dog sitting quietly at the "Stay" command. You will also increase the time you stay away. Always return and give him the great praise and affection he has earned. This exercise will take time, patience and daily practice —but it's worth it.

"*Come*" is probably the most important of all the basic commands. Puppy knows what it means, and he responds to it when and if the spirit moves him. Now he must learn that "Come" means *right now*.

Place him in the "Sit" position on your left side, the leash loose in your right hand. Command "Stay," walk to the end of the leash and turn to face him. After a count of ten or fifteen, say "Andy, come" in a pleasant tone of voice. Then command him to "Sit" in front of and facing you. You want him to come directly and quickly; if he doesn't seem to get the idea, give a light tug on the leash as you give the command. You also want him to sit for a moment, squarely facing you. He is learning to come at once and to wait for further instructions.

After he sits for a few moments, pat him, praise him and let him nose around freely on the end of his leash. Then repeat the "Come" and "Sit" commands. Repeat and repeat and repeat until, at the word "Come," he invariably walks directly to you and sits squarely in front of you without further command.

When puppy has mastered these four basic lessons, he will be a civilized canine citizen, welcome in any society. He will also be an even closer companion to you, his trusted trainer.

LOOKING AHEAD

At the end of a year he's not a baby any more. He's still full of mischief on occasion, but he's growing out of his adolescence and shaping up into a fine, well-behaved animal. He's a much-loved member of the family now. At times he seems "almost human."

But he's not human. The dog has a remarkable ability to learn, but he can't reason. Your pup's behavior habits have been, and always will be, largely shaped and governed by you. It's up to you to see that his behavior is such that he is a courteous and acceptable canine citizen, not only in your household, but in your neighborhood and community.

Learn the leash laws of your area and obey them. They're designed to make it possible for man and dog to live together in a crowded society. There must always be room for dogs. They give so much to all of us in devotion, loyalty and companionship that the world would seem a lonely place without them. The dog will do his part if we'll do ours, so here are some reminders about your lifelong responsibility as a pet owner:

Don't let your dog be a neighborhood bum. You may think he's such an appealing and friendly little fellow that "everybody loves him." Maybe, but not if the friendly little fellow soils your neighbors' lawns, tramples their flower beds, topples their garbage cans, defecates on sidewalks, and gives every passing car and bicycle a merry chase. Confining your dog is a matter of common courtesy to your neighbors. It is also the best way to keep him safe.

Don't let your dog become a habitual barker or howler. Excessive barking can, indeed must, be trained out of him whenever the habit begins to develop. Don't let your dog terrorize mailmen, meter readers and other callers, even if you know he's all bluff. "Don't worry, he won't bite" is not always reassuring and not always true.

Don't let your dog foul city sidewalks. This is one of the biggest problems in urban areas and one of the strongest arguments against big dogs as city pets. Some cities in Europe and South America are even experimenting with outdoor toilets—confined areas covered with sand—for dogs. This could be a solution in the future. Meanwhile, the least you can do is exercise your pet *on the leash only*, and lead him directly to the curb when necessary.

Have your female dog spayed. Don't let her have a litter unless you're sure you can place every one of the pups in a good home. Pet overpopulation is becoming critical. There may be 70 million dogs and cats in the United States now, and it is estimated that at the present rate of increase this figure may reach 200 million within another decade. We are a nation of animal lovers. But there is a cruel and tragic side to our pet picture: Nearly 13 million unwanted dogs and cats are destroyed annually at public and private shelters. Don't take the chance of adding a single puppy to the population of helpless and homeless animals.

Give your dog good health care. You may think that's taken for granted, but it shouldn't be. Always remember that the dog has special needs and that he is dependent on you to keep him sound and healthy. He needs the specialized medical skills of the veterinarian—for preventive immunization, for care when he's ill or injured, for easing the aches and pains of advancing age. He needs a balanced, nutritious diet, specially formulated for dogs, not for humans. He needs to be kept clean and well-groomed; this, too, is a part of good health.

Give your dog love and companionship. His happiness absolutely depends upon you. You are his whole world now. Show your affection often, play with him every day, take him on long walks regularly, pat him and praise him. These are the things he counts on, to reassure him that he is loved. Let him be your best friend; he's going to add much joy to your life in the years to come.

Good health and long life to you both!

VITAL STATISTICS
AND HEALTH RECORD

Your Dog's
Picture

Dog's full name_____

Nickname_____

OWNER

Name_____

Telephone_____

Address_____

_____

VETERINARIAN

Name_____

Telephone_____

Address_____

_____

BACKGROUND DATA

Date of birth_____

Date acquired_____

Description

    Breed_____Sex_____

    Weight_____Height_____

    Color and Markings_____

    _____

    _____

Where obtained_____

_____

Sire_____

Dam_____

Registration Number_____

License Number_____

Notes_____

_____

_____

_____

_____

HEALTH RECORD

First Examination

    Date_____

    Notes_____

_____

Immunization

    Temporary_____

_____

Vaccinations

    Canine Parvovirus (CPV)—date_____

    Distemper—date_____

    Hepatitis—date_____

    Leptospirosis—date_____

    Parainfluenza_____

    Rabies—date_____

    Reminder notes_____

Worming

    Dates_____

    Types of Worms_____
               (identified by veterinarian)

    Medicine_____
            (prescribed by veterinarian)

Other illnesses_____

_____

FEEDING AND GROWTH RECORD

Daily Feedings	Amount	No. of feedings
6 weeks		
2 months		
3 months		
4 months		
6 months		
8 months		
1 year		
Feeding notes		

Growth	Weight	Height
6 weeks		
2 months		
3 months		
4 months		
6 months		
8 months		
1 year		

INDEX